THE WORSH

I enthusiastically recommend Kenny Lamm's *The Worship Ministry Guidebook: Engaging Your Congregation in Transformational Worship*. As one of the most prolific and highly respected worship proponents today, Lamm draws from his extensive experience as a worship leader, mentor, teacher, and consultant to offer guidance that is both highly practical and biblically grounded. He's also thorough, ranging from foundations of worship and worship leadership to worship planning, from leading a worship service to worship evaluation. Whether you're a beginner or a seasoned veteran, **The Worship Ministry Guidebook will be an invaluable resource to you and your ministry for years to come.**

    Scott Shepherd, Worship and Music Specialist, Tennessee Baptist Mission Board

The Worship Ministry Guidebook is a phenomenal resource for current worship leaders, and a special tool for the training of young worship leaders. I have always been impressed by the work and ministry of Kenny Lamm, but this is gold! It is a compilation of wisdom from many of the absolute best worship contributors compiled into one readable and memorable source, along with Kenny's experience and guidance. **I plan to use this for my students!** I believe that every worship pastor currently serving in leadership in any church, any style, any size, as well as those who are preparing for ministry, will be challenged and equipped with wisdom that will help each of us succeed in our God-called journey.

    Larry Grayson, Chair, Department of Worship Studies,
Ouachita Baptist University

Where was this book when I was starting ministry?! Seriously – every minister of music, worship leader, and pastor would benefit greatly from *The Worship Ministry Guidebook*. Kenny Lamm shares his journey and passion for ministry and gives sound and practical advice for those engaged in worship and music ministry – no matter what style or size of your church or ministry. Timely, engaging, and helpful in every way, this book should be on your desk – not your bookshelf.

    Dr. Randy C. Lind, Worship and Music Ministry Partner, Oklahoma Baptists;
Director, Singing Churchmen and Singing Churchwomen of Oklahoma

As a young worship leader, I followed Kenny's blog posts for inspiration and advice that contributed greatly to my development. Having a comprehensive resource like this **is an invaluable tool for any worship leader** of any church, regardless of size or style.

    Kevin Ferstl, Director of Worship and Communication, Church Forward

Practical. Practical. Practical. Kenny Lamm has spent a lifetime training worship leaders, and now he has put into words what has made him so successful in doing so. I know **that any pastor, worship minister, or church leader would find great insights and advice in leading their congregation in worship**. Kenny's awareness and application of Scripture is what helps the most. I will use this as a resource for ALL Kentucky Baptist Churches."

Jason Bubba Stewart, Worship and Music Consultant,
Kentucky Baptist Convention

Planning, preparing, and leading worship requires both skill and heart. This book provides invaluable insights, practical tips, and helpful tools to guide worship leaders in creating meaningful and transformative worship experiences. **Whether you're a seasoned worship leader or just starting out, this book will inspire and equip you to lead with excellence and authenticity.**

Rhon Carter, Worship and Music Catalyst, Georgia Baptist Mission Board

Like a well-trained, sure-handed surgeon, Kenny brilliantly walks through the intricacies of understanding biblical worship and the role of the worship leader. From styles of worship to introducing new songs, no stone is left unturned. **Reading this book will help every person in worship ministry learn how to engage their congregation in the type of worship that leads to life transformation.**

Matt Freeman, Director of Worship and Music,
South Carolina Baptist Convention

One of the most vital things in church life is congregational participation during worship. It's an instant snapshot into a church's health. My friend, Kenny Lamm, addresses the challenge of engaging the congregation for worship head-on in this book. *The Worship Ministry Guidebook* is a vital resource for all worship pastors. In our close-knit group of Baptist state denominational worship directors, we affectionately call Kenny, our 'President' with good reason. Kenny is a great resource for worship pastors and has many hands-on tips, including important foundations for selecting and teaching congregational songs. **I highly recommend this book for current and future worship leaders.**

Tom Tillman, Director of Music and Worship, Texas Baptists

Outstanding text, essential reading for today's worship ministries! Kenny Lamm writes with wisdom and clarity, and doesn't miss a detail. We need to listen to his heart for the Lord's church, a seasoned perspective of a respected leader who is missional and next-gen focused.

Dr. Slater Murphy, Director, Worship Ministries, Mississippi Baptist Convention

Very thoughtful, concise, practical, and easy to read!

Karen Gosselin, Coordinator, State Missionary, Worship Resources,
Alabama State Board of Missions

THE
WORSHIP
MINISTRY
guidebook

ENGAGING YOUR CONGREGATION
IN TRANSFORMATIONAL WORSHIP

KENNY LAMM

 **WorshipLink** PUBLISHING

NC BAPTISTS

Book cover and interior design by Carlee Hoopes www.carleealexandria.com

Publisher's Cataloging-in-Publication Data

Names: Lamm, Kenny, author.
Title: The worship ministry guidebook: engaging your congregation in transformational worship / Kenny Lamm.
Description: Sanford, NC: WorshipLink Publishing, 2023. | Includes bibliographical references.
Identifiers: LCCN: 2023910922 | ISBN: 979-8-9884323-0-2 (paperback)
Subjects: LCSH Public worship | Public worship—Planning | Public worship—Handbooks, manuals, etc.| BISAC RELIGION / Christian Rituals & Practice / Worship & Liturgy | MUSIC / Religious / Christian
Classification: LCC BV15 .L36 2023 | DDC 264—dc23

CONTENTS

CONTENTS

Introduction

A re you frustrated with the lack of participation in your congregation's worship? Do you often feel people are just going through the motions without connecting to God in worship? You are not alone: congregations all over the world are experiencing a sense of spectatorship in worship. What can we as worship leaders do to counteract these trends? How can we lead our churches into passionate, wholehearted, participative worship? How do we truly engage our congregations in transformational worship—worship that makes disciples? In the pages of this book, I hope to take you on a journey that will answer these questions and many more.

I have had the wonderful opportunity of working with churches in the United States and internationally for over 20 years. Before I began traveling extensively connecting with the church worldwide, I had assumed that the worship issues of the American church were probably not global issues. Surely the churches in China, Malaysia, Cuba, Cambodia, Singapore, Argentina, Brunei, or other countries would not encounter conflict in worship or disparity between the generations. Surely there would not be conflict over the instrumentation used in worship. Surely there would not be a trend toward creating spectators in the church.

As I encountered brothers and sisters around the U.S. and internationally, I found that we are remarkably the same in our worship issues. Personal preferences are pervasive in struggles over how churches go about their implementation of congregational worship.

I see churches that have not changed in decades. Many of these are dying because what used to be meaningful worship that engaged the people has now turned into a lifeless ritual.

In many modern churches, I've seen the breeding of a culture of spectators by providing a performance-based event, rather than true worship. People often stand and watch what is happening on stage without being actively involved in worship.

Some churches engage in what has become more of a playlist style of worship. The worship team chooses three popular songs and puts together incredible arrangements of them. In the service, they welcome the people, "turn on" the playlist to run the three songs, and then pass the service on to the pastor for the sermon. Too often, there is no intentional discipleship, no direction, no flow, and these services have become too trite, redundant, and mechanistic.

In many churches that are seeking to be unified across the generations, I see worship conflict over nonessential things in worship (like pulpits or attire) and quarreling about styles of music.

I believe a huge mission for worship leaders around the world is that of helping the church get back on track with God-honoring worship that sets an environment that helps people encounter the transforming power of God—an environment that changes worship spectators into worship participants. The material you hold in your hands will tackle this problem head-on.

Worship and missions are the priorities of the church! They are the most important things we do. My two greatest passions in ministry are worship and missions. I was privileged to serve as a missions and worship pastor for many years—a great combination because the two areas work hand in hand. John Piper points out that "worship is the goal and the fuel of missions:"

> *Missions exists because worship doesn't. Missions is our way of saying: the joy of knowing Christ is not a private, or tribal, or national or ethnic privilege. It is for all. And that's why we go. Because we have tasted the joy of worshipping Jesus, and we want all the families of the earth included.*
>
> *"All the ends of the earth shall remember and turn to the Lord, and all the families of the nations shall worship before you." (Psalm 22:27)*
>
> *Seeking the worship of the nations is fueled by the joy of our own worship. You can't commend what you don't cherish. You can't proclaim what you don't prize. Worship is the fuel and the goal of missions.[1]*

God created us for the ultimate priority of worshipping Him. *The Westminster Shorter Catechism* states, "The chief end of man is to glorify God and enjoy Him forever." I believe vital worship is what fuels everything else the church does. Until we get our worship in a healthy place, we are just sounding gongs and clashing cymbals. When we get our worship right, the other functions of the church will have the fuel they need to fall into place.

Unfortunately, in many of our churches, What God intended for His glory and for our corporate and personal growth—worship—has been transformed from a soul-deep commitment to an ugly, carnal fight.[2]

The journey we will be taking together through this book, I believe, will help you as a worship leader to transform the worship in your church—moving worship from a spectator orientation to one where people are wholeheartedly engaged in worship that transforms disciples.

There are a lot of pieces to put together, beginning with the foundations of worship and worship leadership. Once those foundations are laid, we will build upon them an understanding of all that goes into planning worship services that truly engage the people, disciple the people, and bring to the forefront the glory of God. Then we will dive deeply into how we execute the worship plan with thorough preparation and leadership. We never improve if evaluation is not part of the plan, so we will discuss things we need to do to keep growing in our leadership, utilizing an important evaluative tool.

The book you have in your hands represents over two decades of refining a global curriculum for worship leaders to help them fulfill the calling God has placed on their lives. Throughout the pages of this book, you will see reflection questions pertaining to the material you just read. Be sure to stop and answer those questions. You may be tempted to skip over them to continue reading, but you will miss out on what God may want to show you. These questions will help you connect your life and ministry with the material.

I firmly believe many of the ills of the church's worship today can unknowingly be the fault of worship leaders who may have great intentions but do not realize their practices are hurting worship. These pages will help identify those issues and propose a cure.

Today, some people just go to church out of habit without really offering their worship to God. So what is the difference in just going to church and in coming to offer worship to our God? In her book, *The Worship Architect*, Constance Cherry writes:

> When all is said and done, worship is about experiencing the living God. To experience God is to participate in a conversation with God. It is very different than merely "going to church." Going to church suggests passive worship; coming to offer worship suggests engagement with the God who awaits your presence. Authors Annie Dillard and James Magaw put it very well:[3]
>
> If you ask me why I go to church, I could start with these reasons:
> - To feel better;
> - To be with people whose company I enjoy;
> - To learn about Jesus;
> - To show which side I'm on;
> - To keep people from asking why I missed;
> - To sing my favorite old hymns;
> - To be inspired, taught, and challenged by the sermon.
>
> But if you ask me why I worship, you raise the discussion to another plane. … It calls to memory the words of Annie Dillard, as she writes about worship, 'Does anyone have the foggiest idea what sort of power we so blithely invoke? … The churches are children playing on the floor with their chemistry sets, mixing up a batch of TNT to kill a Sunday morning. It is madness to wear ladies' straw hats and velvet hats to church; we should all be wearing crash helmets. Ushers should issue life preservers and

signal flares; they should lash us to our pews. For the sleeping god may wake someday and take offense, or the waking god may draw us out to where we can never return.'[4]

Don't underestimate the power of worship to transform lives. Don't put worship in a box and try to control it—be flexible as God moves in your church's worship services. James Magaw says it this way:

When I worship, I expose myself to the power of God without any personal control over the outcome. Sometimes it brings healing, peace, forgiveness, confrontation, or hope. Always it calls me to move beyond the farthest point I have yet reached, and pushes me into uncharted territories. Going to church is easy most days. Worship is another matter. It is an awesome thing to know oneself fallen into the hands of the living God.[5]

BEFORE YOU DIVE IN

Take time to pray before you read each portion of the book; ask God to reveal ways that He would have you change or ways you need to adjust the worship ministry of your church. Highlight the pages. Take notes of everything that God places on your heart that needs addressing. Every time I teach this material, God shows me places I have failed or taken shortcuts rather than truly creating the best worship services to engage the church. We are all works in progress.

I have prayed and continue to pray that God will impact every life that encounters this book. Don't rush through this material. Fully digest each section and determine how that material can help you be the worship leader God has called you to be.

I thank God for you!

Understanding Worship

To be effective worship leaders, we must first set the foundations upon which we will build all our practical skills in planning and leading worship. We must thoroughly understand these basics of worship and the principles of worship leadership before we can plan and lead worship that will effectively catalyze and transform a congregation to be participative and, at the same time, disciple them to be more like Christ.

WHAT IS WORSHIP?

Merriam-Webster Dictionary defines *worship* in a couple of ways. The more generic definition is "To regard with great or extravagant respect, honor, or devotion."[6]

We must realize that everyone is a worshipper. We all focus our respect, honor, or devotion on something in our lives. Worship is about saying that this person, thing, or experience means more to me than anything else. It is the thing of highest value in my life. That "thing" might be a relationship, a goal I am seeking, a status I desire or have, a possession I love, a career I have thrown myself into, some pleasure I crave, or perhaps an addiction such as pornography, substances, gambling, or social media. It might be my family. Whatever the object of my devotion may be, it is the thing that I have concluded in my heart that means the most to me.

Every person—Christian or non-believer—is a worshipper. Whatever a person values most represents what that person worships. You can trace how a person spends their time, attention, money, thoughts, conversations, etc., to see what that person truly worships.

You can see worship powerfully displayed at a ball game or a concert. You may go to a Buddhist temple or an athletic stadium and see great worship. In so many places, you can see passionate worship displayed. But what is so discouraging is that it seems the people in those venues are far more moved by the little gods they worship than Christians are by the Savior of our souls, the Creator of the universe, even though we worship the true God.

You see, basically, people are great worshippers; it's just that the OBJECT of their worship is misdirected. We need to ask, "Who or what are we worshipping?"

Misdirected worship focuses on idols in our lives. Tim Keller speaks about idols:

> *An idol is anything more important to you than God, anything that absorbs your heart and imagination more than God, anything you seek to give you what only God can give.*
>
> *A counterfeit god is anything so central and essential to your life that, should you lose it, your life would feel hardly worth living. An idol has such a controlling position in your heart that you can spend most of your passion and energy, your emotional and financial resources, on it without a second thought.*
>
> *An idol is whatever you look at and say, in your heart of hearts, "If I have that, then I'll feel my life has meaning, then I'll*

know I have value, then I'll feel significant and secure." There are many ways to describe that kind of relationship to something, but perhaps the best one is worship.[7]

Harold Best defines worship in this broad sense as "acknowledging that someone or something else is greater – worth more – and by consequence, to be obeyed, feared, and adored. … Worship is the sign that in giving myself completely to someone or something, I want to be mastered by it."[8]

Indeed, whatever rules our hearts and lives will master us. Jesus said it very clearly in Matthew 6:21, "For where your treasure is, there your heart will be also."

What we set our affections upon shapes us into whom we will become. **Worship is transformative.**

> **Take a moment to examine your own life. Where do your affections lie? Are you serving an idol? Do you need to transform your life to place Christ in His rightful place once again?**

A second definition of worship hones in on a more spiritual object: "To honor or show reverence for as a divine being or supernatural power."[9]

As worship leaders, not only do we need to align our affections to place God as the object of our worship, but we must also strive to create and lead worship services that will help people realign their affections—to help them put Jesus back on the throne of their lives, and to make God the object of their affections. This is transformational worship. We will explore this much more as we continue.

As we begin to get a good definition of biblical worship, we must come to terms with the fact that the Bible does not give us a formal definition of worship.

The English word, *worship*, comes from the Anglo-Saxon word, *weorthscipe*. *Weorth* means "worth," and *scipe* means "shape" or "quality." Combined, they take on the meaning of "having worth" or "ascribing worth." In our services of worship, we declare God's worth—we praise Him, honor Him, and talk of His attributes. We get a glimpse of this purpose in 1 Peter 2:9:

> *But you are a chosen race, a royal priesthood, a holy nation, a people for his own possession, that you may proclaim the excellencies of him who called you out of darkness into his marvelous light.*

We declare the worth of God—that He alone is the object of our affection. Worship is the revelation of who God is and our response to that revelation.

Although the Bible does not give us a definition of worship, there are two significant *kinds* of words for worship described by Dr. Michael Morrison:

> *The first means to bow down, to kneel, to put one's face down as an act of respect and submission. Our body language is saying, "I will do whatever you want me to. I am ready to listen to your instructions and I am willing to obey." The other kind of biblical word means to serve. Roughly half of the time these words are translated as worship, and the other half as serve. It carries the idea of doing something for God — making a sacrifice or carrying out his instructions.[10]*

We can also consider these two categories as *acts of reverence* and *acts of service*. Upon deeper study, you will see that the biblical words indicate that worship is very physical—prostrating oneself, bowing down, stooping low, kneeling, etc.

The most common word for worship in Greek is προσκυνέω (*proskuneó*). It means "by kneeling or prostration to do homage (to one) or make obeisance, whether in order to express respect or to make supplication."[11]

The most common Hebrew word for worship in the Bible is *shachah*. Its meaning is "to bow down, prostrate oneself … before God in worship."[12]

Both the most common Hebrew and Greek words denote physical activity in worship.

John Piper describes worship this way:

> *The inner essence of worship is to know God truly and then respond from the heart to that knowledge by valuing God, treasuring God, prizing God, enjoying God, being satisfied with God above all earthly things. And then that deep, restful, joyful satisfaction in God overflows in demonstrable acts of praise from the lips and demonstrable acts of love in serving others for the sake of Christ.[13]*

As Piper indicates, worship should be a revelation and response experience. Warren Wiersbe writes:

> *Worship is the believer's response of all that they are – mind, emotions, will, body – to what God is and says and does.[14]*

We respond with our entire being to the revelation of God. As worship leaders, we need to be sure we are showing forth an accurate and beautiful revelation of God in the services we lead and plan. Revealing God in His fullness is necessary for transformational worship.

Robert Schaper further drills down into this idea of revelation and response:

> *Worship is the expression of a relationship in which God the Father reveals himself and his love in Christ, and by His Holy Spirit administers grace to which we respond in faith, gratitude, and obedience.[15]*

Steven Brooks expounds on Schaper's quote:

> *First, notice that in our worship, God desires to have a relationship with us. He loves for us to be in his presence. Next, Schaper rightly mentions the revelation and response of worship. The word of God is proclaimed to the Christian community as an intentional presentation of the truth about the triune God— Father, Son, Holy Spirit—and God's relationship with his people (revelation); and there is a reply of God's people to the truth proclaimed shown by means of a prepared or spontaneous opportunity for the worshippers to answer, reply, or react (response). Our worship should be a response to what God has done, is doing and will do in our lives.[16]*

God initiates worship by revealing Himself to us. Michael Morrison writes about how we respond to that revelation:

> *Our worship is a response to what God has revealed himself to be, not only in who he is, but also in what he has done and is doing and will do in the future. Worship includes all our responses to God – including a response with our mind, such as our belief in God's worthiness, our emotions, such as love and trust, and our actions and our words. Our heart expresses itself in words and songs; our mind is active when we want to learn what God*

wants us to do, and our bodies and strength are involved when we obey and when we serve.[17]

Bob Kauflin has written an excellent definition of worship along with a detailed scriptural basis of the writing that deserves our study.[18] I encourage you to take some time to examine this closely:

> *Christian worship is the response of God's redeemed people to His self-revelation that exalts God's glory in Christ in our minds, affections and wills, in the power of the Holy Spirit.*
>
> **Christian worship** … is different from every kind of worship because it has been made possible through Jesus Christ (Revelation 5:9-10).
>
> **Is the response** … God has already done something outside of us and inside of us that enables us to worship Him. We are not the initiators of worship; God is (Acts 17:24-31).
>
> **Of God's redeemed people** … Just as God delivered the nation of Israel from Egypt to worship Him (Exodus 8:1), so He has redeemed us as a holy nation to declare His praises (1 Peter 2:9). Worship of God is intended to be corporate, not simply personal.
>
> **To his self-revelation** … we can't know God apart from Him revealing Himself to us. He has shown Himself to us in creation, His Word, and ultimately His Son (Romans 1:20; Hebrews 1:1-4).
>
> **That exalts** … the essence of worship is exalting—raising up, lifting high, submitting to, magnifying, making much of, honoring, reverencing, celebrating—the triune God (Psalm 71:19).
>
> **God's glory in Christ** … Moses asked God to show him

His glory and God passed before him and proclaimed His nature (Exodus 34:6-7). God has enabled us to see His glory in the face of Christ (2 Corinthians 4:6).

In our minds … worship involves thinking, meditating, reflecting, processing, evaluating, understanding what God has revealed to us of Himself (Romans 12:1-2; Psalms 111:2).

Affections … true worship involves the heart as well as the head. We worship what we love and value the most (Matthew 22:37-38).

And wills … If we are truly worshipping God, we will truly be transformed (2 Corinthians 3:17-18). Our choices will reflect our profession that God is supreme in our lives (Romans 12:1-2).

In the power of the Holy Spirit … We are those who worship by the Spirit of God and depend on His leading and enabling (Philippians 3:3).

> Spend some time going back through these definitions of worship. Write a definition of worship you can tell others when they ask, "What is worship?".

OUR WORSHIP MUST BE TRINITARIAN BUT CHRIST-CENTERED

Christian worship must honor the Father as we worship the Son by the power of the Spirit. The concept of Trinitarian worship can be a bit confusing because of the complexity of understanding the Trinity. Many of our songs mention the Father, Son, and Holy Spirit. Our prayers may be Trinitarian. Creeds talk of the Trinity. Yet it is of most importance for our services to be Christ-centered. Our worship should tell the gospel story. The gospel is transformative.

Bryan Chapell, in his book, *Christ-Centered Worship*, makes this concept clear:

> *We make our worship Christ-centered not by failing to mention Father or Spirit, but by honoring them with the gospel pattern that reflects their will and purpose. We honor the Father when we sing of his greatness to humble hearts and prepare them to receive the grace that Christ provides. And were we not to mention the provision of Christ, then we would have demeaned the God who sent him no matter how much more praise we heaped upon the Father. Similarly, we honor the Spirit when we call on him to help us understand Scripture's testimony of Christ's work. And we would grieve the Spirit if we were to make him, whose ministry is testifying of Christ, the chief object of our worship ... We make our worship Christ-centered not by simply mentioning the name of Jesus, and definitely not by failing to honor the Father and the Spirit; we make our worship Christ-centered by shaping it to help God's people understand and appreciate the grace in all Scripture that culminates in their Savior's ministry.[19]*

If our services are to be Christ-centered, that causes tension when we think of ways that we often deviate from a focus on Jesus in our services. There are times when we celebrate Mother's Day, Father's Day, patriotic holidays, and similar occasions. While it is great to honor our mothers and fathers and celebrate our country, many churches often spend significant amounts of time taking the focus away from Christ in our services. This should not be the case in our corporate worship services. We must always seek to keep Christ at the center of these times of deviating from corporate worship and keep these non-biblical celebrations to a minimum.

> **Examine several weeks of past worship services. Do you see a Trinitarian but Christ-centered approach to these services? Do you spend too much time on worldly foci?**

Morrison describes three kinds of worship—worship that involves speaking, listening, and doing. All three areas are vital to corporate worship services. This further illustrates the whole-life effect of corporate worship that should yield the result of lifestyle worship—worshipping and serving God with our whole life throughout the day.

> *There is a worship that expresses the heart, and worship that involves the mind, and a worship that involves the body. There is a worship that is giving praise upward, a worship that is receiving instructions from above, and a worship that carries out instruction in the world around us. We need all three types of worship. Some people focus primarily on speaking or singing praise to God. Praise is good, but if all we do is praise God, without ever listening to what he says, we have to ask whether we believe the words we are saying. If he is really all wise and all loving, then we need to be attentive to what he is telling us, because he is worth listening to.*

Similarly, all talk and no action does not show God the respect he deserves. Actions speak louder than words, and if our behavior isn't changed by God, then our actions are saying that God isn't important — he's a nice idea, but not relevant to our day-to-day lives. When we really believe that God is worthy of every praise, then we will be willing to listen and to change the way we live in response to such a worthy God. We will trust him and seek him and want to please him as much as we can. Worship should affect our behavior.[20]

PERSONAL WORSHIP AND CORPORATE (GATHERED) WORSHIP

Worship can be experienced in two primary ways—(1) **personal worship** and (2) **corporate (or gathered) worship**. Personal worship is when you spend intimate times of worship with just you and God. Corporate worship is worship offered by you and one or more others.

PERSONAL WORSHIP

Personal worship can be experienced in one of two ways:

1. WORSHIP IN SOLITUDE

First, when we are alone with God to commune with Him, read His Word, and pray, we can describe that as **worship in solitude**. Jesus consistently demonstrated the necessity of spending time alone with His Father. This is a necessary part of the Christian's life, to set our heart and affections on God in a one-on-One manner each day, allowing God to speak to us through His Word and prayer. This time alone with God fuels our life with Christ.

2. LIFESTYLE WORSHIP

As Morrison pointed out in the three kinds of worship, one type of worship involves our day-to-day lives, trusting God, seeking Him, and wanting to please Him in all we do. The second way we experience personal worship can be called **lifestyle worship**. I Corinthians 10:31 speaks to this:

> So, whether you eat or drink, or whatever you do, do all to the glory of God.

Also, Micah 6:8 says,

> He has told you, O man, what is good; and what does the Lord require of you but to do justice, and to love kindness, and to walk humbly with your God?

Richard Foster, in his book, *Celebration of Discipline*, speaks of lifestyle worship: "Just as worship begins in holy expectancy, it ends in holy obedience. If worship does not propel us into greater obedience, it has not been worship."[21]

As growing disciples of Christ, our lives should conform to look more like Jesus daily. This is played out in our lives of worship and service.

CORPORATE (GATHERED) WORSHIP

Corporate worship is when individuals come together with others to offer their worship to God. Martin Luther stated, "To gather with God's people in united adoration of the Father is as necessary to the Christian life as prayer."

Steven Brooks says this about corporate worship,

> *In corporate worship, gathered Christians reflect the very nature of the triune God, simultaneously singular and plural, and*

experience God corporately through both the presence of the Holy Spirit, and through one another. There is also a dual audience in corporate worship, reflected in Paul's writings to the Ephesians: 'Speak to one another with psalms, hymns and spiritual songs. Sing and make music in your heart to the Lord, always giving thanks to God the Father for everything, in the name of our Lord Jesus Christ,' (Ephesians 5:19–20). We sing to God and to one another." [22]

This passage brings up an important point that is vastly overlooked today. Gathered worship has a horizontal and a vertical element. Not only is our worship directed to God as we offer Him our praise and worship, giving thanks for all He has done, it also requires us to "speak to one another" in declaring His worth, testifying of His goodness, etc. Gathered worship has a communal aspect that differentiates it from personal worship. In addition, I have found that experiencing the people around me in worship can encourage me to worship more wholeheartedly. It is moving to come to worship and see a family present who has just lost a loved one, and to see them worshipping with all their might; it really encourages those around them. Seeing a grandmother, daughter, and granddaughter standing side by side, boldly singing songs to the Lord together motivates others to worship wholeheartedly. The communal aspect of corporate worship cannot be understated. It is vital to our lives to have that interaction in worship.

WRONGLY CHANGING GATHERED WORSHIP TO PERSONAL WORSHIP

Too often, in many instances of "contemporary worship,"

churches transform their times of gathered worship into personal worship for the congregation by turning the lights down, so you don't see anyone around you, and by having the sound so loud that you cannot hear those in your area. Essentially it denies the existence of the corporate body journeying together in this act of worship when you cannot see nor hear your fellow worshippers. There have been times I have had congregations turn and face one another as they sing a song of testimony, declaring the worth of God to each other; this helps them recognize that they are in this together. We can exhort, encourage, comfort, and so much more in the gathered horizontal aspect of worship.

> **Too often, worshippers engage in personal worship in a gathered worship setting. How are we, as worship leaders, causing this problem? How can we combat this problem?**

HOW PERSONAL WORSHIP FEEDS CORPORATE WORSHIP

I must pause here to point out a few things about personal worship in relation to corporate (gathered) worship.

Our ability to lead in corporate worship greatly depends on our personal walk with God. We cannot lead people to a place we have not been ourselves. We must be experiencing God in worship throughout the week so we can lead out of an overflow of being with the Master. We can show people the magnificence of God only when we have genuinely experienced it ourselves.

To further illustrate this point, I often show the airline safety video excerpt of the oxygen masks dropping down in case of an emergency on an airliner. The flight attendant says, "You need to put your oxygen mask on first before attempting to help those around you." We as worship leaders must be plugged into the oxygen—the power of God—through worship before we can help others with their oxygen masks—their experiences in gathered worship.

Personal worship is a prerequisite to corporate worship. The previous explanation discusses how this is true for worship leaders, but think of how important this is for the congregants. If they are not experiencing God through times of personal worship throughout the week, they will not likely bring a great sacrifice of praise and worship to the corporate setting every week. This leads to the following statement:

You should come worshipping to church, not come to church to worship. Only when we come out of a worship-filled week, already worshipping, do we arrive at church ready to participate in a great time of praising and worshipping our God. When, on the other hand, we come out of a dry spell of personal worship, we have little to give and essentially begin the gathered time of worship from an empty tank.

> How does the personal worship life of the individuals in your congregation influence times of gathered worship? How does your personal worship life affect your ability to lead worship? If your church can help people improve their lives of personal worship, how would it benefit your church's gathered worship?

FOUR CONTEXTS OF WORSHIP

Worship occurs in differing groupings of people that we will call "contexts." We will look at these four contexts and determine how each one benefits our lives of worship corporately and personally. Each context is uniquely different, and worship leaders should be acutely aware of their benefits and the characteristics that make them unique. (These ideas were first espoused by Syd Hielema and then further expanded by Paul Clark, Jr. I have made adaptions as well. For an excellent expansion on these contexts, check out Steven Brooks' book, *Worship Quest*.[23])

1. PRIVATE WORSHIP (WORSHIP IN SOLITUDE)

Private worship is when it is just you and God spending time together in worship. This is the context in which personal worship in solitude takes place. It might express itself in a scheduled time of praying and reading the Bible each morning, singing worship songs during your morning commute, or backpacking in the mountains and communing with God as you find time away from the busyness of life. In private worship, you are making time with God a priority, a time to fuel your soul with His presence. Psalm 46:10 says, "Be still and know that I am God." Life today, unfortunately, is at such a pace that many Christians neglect this vital context of worship. As I mentioned in the section on personal worship, private worship helps us prepare for times of worship with other believers.

Are you regularly engaged in times of worship in solitude? Are you encouraging those under your care to do the same?

2. SMALL GROUP WORSHIP

In this context, small groups of people familiar with one another come together and worship, whether as the primary objective or as a part of another gathering. Some examples may be people gathering together for a game night at your home and people having a time of prayer and/or singing together; coworkers gathering 30 minutes before the start of a workday for some devotional time together; a family gathering together for Bible reading and prayer each day; and a church small group gathering for Bible study, prayer, and singing. There are many small group worship contexts within your church, such as a men's or ladies' group, Celebrate Recovery, Sunday School groups, discipleship groups, and others. We worship leaders have opportunities to encourage small group worship in numerous extensions of the worship ministry, such as the worship team, choirs, and tech teams. Just as private worship helps people prepare for corporate/ gathered worship, so does small group worship. These small groups provide opportunities for intimate prayer, study, and singing and are also great environments for accountability and discipleship.

Sid Hielema makes these observations about this worship context:

The central distinguishing feature of (small group) worship is its ability to deepen interpersonal relationships. It's easy to get lost in a 250-member congregation on Sunday morning, but no one is overlooked in the (small group) setting. These settings allow us to become transparent and vulnerable. In that transparency, we come to see more clearly both the presence of God's grace and of pain and brokenness in each one's life. When permission to be vulnerable is given in these settings, community is built and the worship becomes a vehicle for placing all of the activities of this particular extended family group inside the gracious presence of God. I recall once directing our church choir as we were rehearsing a chorus from Handel's Messiah one December. While we sang, an alto in the second row began weeping silently, and we knew why: her brother had died at an early age just three weeks before and the music had allowed her grief to come to the surface. As we continued to sing, hands next to her held her while other eyes around the room moistened in compassion for her grief and their own now-remembered griefs. We were a choir in rehearsal, but there we also became (small group) at worship.[24]

> **Are you regularly engaged in small group gatherings for worship? These are vital to your spiritual growth. Are you creating worship moments in your settings of the worship ministry beyond just preparing to lead others, i.e., are you leading these small groups to have times of worship either formally or impromptu?**

3. CONGREGATIONAL WORSHIP

Congregational worship is the gathering of the church—the weekly corporate worship gathering. These settings are likely attended by multiple generations and perhaps various ethnicities. There are people with whom you have much in common and people with whom you have little in common. There are close friends and some that you may not get along with in attendance. Congregational worship is the focus of most worship leaders in creating the large weekly gathering. Churches build special meeting places for this context of worship and spend much time and many resources to make this weekly worship service happen. We see the early church gathering for congregational worship, and the practice has continued throughout every century.

The great diversity of people and their life challenges and celebrations make congregational worship perhaps the most challenging of all worship contexts. Worship leaders seek to speak to everyone to help them in their journey of worship despite varying preferences for musical styles and current life situations. Some people are ready to celebrate what God is doing in their lives, while others are going through intense pain and need the comfort that only God can bring. I love this description by Jim Altizer:

> The Apostle Paul described the body of Christ not in a homogeneous way, but as being composed of old and young (Titus 2:2–6); rich and poor (1 Cor 11:21–22); of varied giftedness (1 Cor 12:4); mixed in race, gender and status (Gal 3:28; 1 Cor 12:13). It is tempting to simplify things by narrowing or targeting the population of your Church, but Paul makes the case that homogeneity (sameness) actually cripples the body of Christ (1 Cor 12:19). Unity, on the other hand, verifies both

the Truth and love of God. Unity within diversity is the way of Christ. Consequently, when outsiders see the proverbial ballerina, punked–out teenager, brain surgeon and custodian all worshipping together, they are convinced of the real Jesus, and of his love for his people. They know something supernatural is going on.[25]

We will discuss more about finding unity among this type of diversity later in this book as we talk about unified worship.

4. FESTIVAL WORSHIP

Festival worship is a large gathering of people for an express purpose that is not regular in occurrence. Summer youth camp worship, Promise Keepers rallies filling football stadiums, Passion worship conferences, the Sing! Conference and other similar gatherings reflect the festival worship gathering. Paul Clark, Jr. describes it this way:

. . . there was a celebrity status of platform personalities. At each event, it was likely that the vast majority of the attendees did not know each other, yet shared a common focus that prepared them for a high energy, high adrenaline rush that characterized such gatherings, and may have actually defined them after all was said and done . . . in such gatherings (for the most part), people who have gathered are strangers to each other, and thus have very little relational baggage. Participants know the celebrity leaders by reputation, adding to the expectancy and energy of the gathered crowd, thus affecting each attendee as well. . . .

Festival worship gatherings are sometimes stamped by signature songs or music styles. Attendees expect to participate in singing these tunes as part of the experience, and often come away from the events with the music ringing in their ears and stuck in their head to the extent that hearing it reminds them of the gathering and hopefully of personal commitments made there. The feuds in churches over music styles often point to styles adopted from such events "invading" our church repertoire, the fact is that festival gatherings have influenced congregational worship liturgy for many years[26]

IMPLICATIONS OF THE FOUR CONTEXTS OF WORSHIP

Hielema talks about *festival-envy syndrome*, where people look for festival worship experiences in the other contexts. There is an additional blurring of lines between the four categories as well.

1. Each one of the four contexts has a legitimate, unique, and necessary contribution to make.

The central distinguishing feature of each context is not exclusive to that context: (small group worship) requires faithfulness, congregational worship provides inspiration, and festivals make space for God. However, each context is able to provide one gift to its participants in the strongest, most focused, consistent manner in ways that the others cannot. Each one of the four belongs in the worship life of the Christian community; each is irreplaceable and irreducible.

2. Each context is intended to strengthen one's worship in the other three.

Festival-envy syndrome points to a competition between

these contexts. We see this competition occur in other ways as well: a believer will say, "I don't worship in church on Sundays; I go for a walk in the forest." Another will say, "My real congregation is my prayer group. I feel like a faceless number in the congregation on Sunday." Misunderstanding the chemistry between the four contexts allows such competition to flourish.

Instead, each context strengthens the participant to worship more fully in the other three. The transparency within the (small group) reminds us that all with whom we worship on Sunday morning are fellow children of God who bring their brokenness to God's grace, though it may not be obvious to us in that context. Our times of solitude (private) free us for greater transparency in (small group) settings. The inspiration we receive at festivals nourishes us with hope and energy to continue the journey faithfully in the other three contexts back at home. These four contexts are completely interwoven and mutually reinforcing.

3. Worshippers tend to be the least focused and the least prepared to worship in the congregational context.

One irony that flows from this discussion of four worship contexts is that the congregational setting clocks the most person-hours per week, but it is also susceptible to come out the worst when people practice context confusion. Worshippers frequently hope to receive festival-like inspiration, family-like intimacy, and solitude-like space through their Sunday worship. This hope is maintained by the fact that congregational worship does provide some of these benefits in varying degrees some of the time.[27]

What do these takeaways mean for worship leaders? How do we help congregants understand the different contexts of worship and their purposes? How do we reduce the confusion that we, as worship leaders, are causing in this area (specifically, the blurring of lines between festival worship and congregational worship)?

WORSHIP SPECTATORS OR PARTICIPANTS?

Too often today, our churches take on a performance orientation, feeling like the congregation is a group of spectators watching what is playing out on stage. Rory Noland writes in his book *Worship on Earth as It Is in Heaven*:

> *Modern churchgoers are culturally conditioned and complacent, instead of actively engaged in worship .... Worship has become a spectator sport. Unfortunately, too many of us approach church the same way — as casual observers instead of active participants. We come to listen to the music. We'll join in and sing here and there but we mostly hang back, as if we're spectators observing a performance. We act more like outsiders and newcomers than God's loved children. We plop in the pew and wait for somebody to tell us that to do. The result, more often than not, is lethargic worship as opposed to passionate worship.*[28]

The Bible tells us to "sing and make music in our hearts to the Lord," and it tells us different instruments we can use. We are to lift our hands and clap our hands. The Bible tells us to kneel, bow down, lie prostrate, and shout in worship. We are even told to dance as an expression of our worship. We are told to be participative in worship, not as an option, but as a command. Yet, in so many congregations, worship seems to be just from the neck up; there is no physical expression other than perhaps singing and bowing heads during prayer. Even in the singing, many refuse to participate or barely sing at all. Participation is passive at best.

This gets back to the earlier discussion about the object of our worship. If we worship a ball team when we are in the stadium, we get very physical in our display of loyalty and passion. Our passions are often expressed in our physical actions. The problem is that we often save our passion for other things.

THE AUDIENCE OF ONE ANALOGY

In today's consumeristic mindset, we often see corporate worship in these roles:

- **The people in the congregation are the audience.** They are there to observe what is happening on stage. They have become "pew potatoes" merely observing the "show" produced by the worship leaders.
- **The worship leaders are the actors.** They are performing for the congregation, giving them a quality show. Excellent music and outstanding preaching are the norms.
- **God is the prompter of worship.** He is helping the worship leaders know what songs to sing and helping the pastor know what to expound upon. He directs the actors/worship leaders through the service of worship.

Kierkegaard[29] flipped this around to say that biblical worship should look like this:

- **The people in the congregation are the actors or performers of worship.** They are active participants offering God their wholistic worship—heart, soul, mind, and strength.
- **The worship leaders are the prompters for worship.** They guide this worship journey by planning and leading songs, prayers, Bible reading, ministry times, sermons, the Lord's Supper, etc. Their main objective is to lead the congregation well to voice their worship and praise unhindered.
- **God is the Audience—the Audience of One.** He is receiving our worship and praise. Our praise is a sweet aroma to Him.

This analogy breaks down a bit here because God is more than an Audience—He interacts with the worshippers in times of worship. What this analogy does is rightly help us see that the congregation is to be made up of **active participants** in worship, and the worship leaders (while indeed also worshipping) have a primary obligation to guide the journey of worship to help the congregants to truly worship.

[It should be noted that the creation of an audience culture in the congregation can partly be traced back to the American revivalist period, where evangelistic crusades were mostly a collection of discrete events that entertain or instruct that were emulated by so many Western churches and then broadcast throughout the world through missionaries. Unfortunately, this is not biblical worship and we must seek ways to return worship to the people. Much more will be shared about this in the remainder of the book.]

Brian Crosby of Wayside Presbyterian Church in Signal Mountain, Tennessee, says it so well:

Worship is dialogical — God speaks, and His people respond. Therefore, as active participants in worship, we hear the call of God to worship Him; we engage in various responsive readings from Scripture or a confession of faith; we follow along in the reading of God's Word in our own Bibles; we join our hearts in the prayers that are offered; we take notes (mental or actual) of the points made in the sermon; we sing thoughtfully and joyfully the psalms, hymns, and spiritual songs with grace in our hearts; we confess our sins with a sincere awareness of our depravity; we remember to improve upon our own baptism when we take part in the baptism of another; we participate in the body and blood of Jesus at the Lord's Supper, remembering by faith His sacrifice of atonement for our sins; we actively take comfort in being assured of His pardoning grace; we give of our tithes and offerings as an expression of our thanksgiving toward and dependence on God; and we go with the peace that God has promised in His benediction. In every element, then, we are fully present and attentive.

Being an active participant in worship may involve certain appropriate postures or movements. It's not uncommon to stand for the reading of God's Word out of respect (Neh. 8:5), to bow one's head in humble prayer (Psalms 35:13), or to stretch out one's hands to receive the benediction (Numbers 6:24–26; Nehemiah. 8:6). All these are ways to increase both individual and communal participation in worship.

Rather than being mere observers or passive attenders in the worship of our triune God, may we carefully prepare ourselves for worship, eagerly expect God to be at work among His people in worship, and actively engage our hearts, minds, souls, and strength in each element of worship. And as we become active participants, may God work in us that which is pleasing in His sight, through Jesus Christ, to whom be glory forever and ever (Hebrews 13:21).[30]

> **Do you feel that the people in your church take on the role of spectator more than a performers of worship? What about you? How can we help our people become more demonstrative in the physical aspects of worship?**

WAYS TO ENCOURAGE PHYSICAL EXPRESSION AND FREEDOM IN WORSHIP

Many worshippers are hesitant to express themselves physically in worship for several reasons that include:

1. Fear of what others will think of them
2. Being unaware of the biblical mandates for physical expression
3. Growing up in a church that does not model or even stifles physical expression
4. Feeling that worship should reflect only reverence and awe
5. Association of physical expressions with churches that have vastly different doctrinal views
6. Having no passion in their worship, and perhaps no relationship with God

There are many ways that worship leaders/pastors can encourage physical expression in worship:

1. **Preach and teach on worship.** Whether using full sermons or frequent sound bites in services, worship leaders can point out biblical mandates to be physically involved in worship. Many people are unaware of the biblical imperatives and may feel that being still and reverent is the appropriate way to worship. Therefore it is important to teach the appropriateness of physical expression in worship and how that expression should flow from the heart. While silence and being still is also biblically mandated, they should be a part of a much more extensive repertoire of worship practices.

2. **Practice physical expressions in personal worship.** Many people did not grow up in a church that modeled participation in worship, and may feel uncomfortable involving their bodies in worship. Encouraging people to practice the physical gestures of worship in their personal worship in solitude gives them ways to experience the physical side of worship without fear of people judging them. As they find value in participatory worship in private, they will find themselves more comfortable being expressive in corporate worship settings.

3. **Encourage expression.** The worship leader can read a passage of Scripture to the congregation, for example, exhorting the lifting of hands as an expression of worship, and then encourage the worshippers to lift their hands as they sing the chorus of a suitable song, following the biblical encouragement. This will often give people the freedom to try an expression along with the congregation, without feeling that they will stand out. This should not be a regular exercise, but on occasion, coupled with teaching, it can be effective.

4. **Model physical worship.** As the worship team and choir become demonstrative in their worship, the congregation will become much more comfortable expressing their worship physically. Conversely, when the worship leaders are more stoic in leading worship, the congregation will reflect their lack of involvement. This will be discussed in greater detail later in this book.

5. **The lead pastor models freedom in worship.** The congregation sees their senior pastor as the primary worship leader of the church in many ways. If the pastor is reserved in his worship, the congregation may likely follow along. However, if he is demonstrative, the congregation will feel much greater freedom in worship. I have seen pastors who often are busy reading their sermon notes during the musical portion of worship. This communicates to the congregation that this part of worship is not important. The pastor I served with for many years was a passionate worshipper who was demonstrative and genuine in his worship. This spoke volumes to the congregation who found much more freedom in their worship due to the pastor's modeling of worship practices.

6. **Involve interpretive movement or a dance team in worship.** People with gifts in this area can help worship come alive at times as they interpret the words with physical gestures. Seeing worship enacted this way can lead to more freedom from the congregation.

7. **Involve physical movement as part of the offering, Lord's Supper, or ministry times as people are invited to move**

from their seats to give, partake, and experience various elements of worship. Giving worshippers the opportunity to physically move to carry out acts of worship further involves their bodies in participative worship.

> **Which of these suggestions do you feel you could implement in your setting?**

STYLES OF WORSHIP

Many churches offer two or more styles of worship (generally based on music style preference). In addition, many churches have concurrent worship services for various age groups, separating the children, students, and adults in worship. I refer to the practice of offering a variety of styles of worship as a **food court approach to worship**. In a mall food court, you, your family, and friends can choose to divide up and go to the food vendors that meet your current food preferences, so that everyone is happy with their selection. The same level of satisfaction may not have resulted had you chosen to go to a single restaurant with only one variety of food. So if one person prefers Asian food, another Mexican food, and another Italian food, they can all find fulfillment in a food court that offers all those options. Similarly, a church may provide a traditional service for those who prefer hymns accompanied by an organ and piano, another service for those who love country music led by a country band, and another that is led by a modern worship band leading the top worship songs of the day for those who prefer "contemporary" worship.

There are times when dividing the church by preferential style may be needed—especially in those cases where a church will only remain missional in its setting by offering a style of worship that is quite different from that currently provided and the participants are unwilling to sacrifice personal preferences. However, it is hoped that every reader whose church offers varying styles of worship will fully consider the possibilities of moving to a unified approach to worship, which will be explained as we continue this journey together.

In working with churches over the last 13 years, I have seen many churches which have offered a contemporary and a traditional style of worship who are now desiring to come back together with everyone worshipping in one style of worship. There has been a strong move away from ageism, away from separating and dividing, and back to intergenerational, multi-ethnic worship.

WORSHIP WARS

Take a look at this excerpt from a U.S. newspaper objecting to the new trends in church music (source unknown):

> *There are several reasons for opposing it.*
> *One, it's too new.*
> *Two, it's often worldly, even blasphemous.*
> *The new Christian music is not as pleasant as the more established style.*
> *Because there are so many songs, you can't learn them all.*
> *It puts too much emphasis on instrumental music rather than godly lyrics.*

This new music creates disturbances making people act indecently and disorderly.

The preceding generation got along without it.

It's a money-making scene, and some of these new music upstarts are lewd and loose.

Does this sound like some of the "fan" mail you received the week after you pushed the envelope in worship with some new worship songs?

This was written by a pastor in 1723 attacking Isaac Watts, the writer of great hymns like *When I Survey the Wondrous Cross, Joy to the World, and O God, Our Help in Ages Past.*

You see, "worship wars" are nothing new to our decade. As long as we have had an organized church and people with personal preferences, there has been conflict. As James 4:1 says, "What causes fights and quarrels among you? Don't they come from your desires that battle with you?"

Worship wars have been raging at least since around 700 AD. Here are some highlights outlined by my friend, Steve Hamrick[31]:

- When the Gregorian Chant became the official music of the church, it was characterized by a single monophonic, unaccompanied melody sung only by men. Later young boys with unchanged voices started singing with the men, but their voices were displaced by an octave. There were many who objected. Later harmony was added to the music of the church, but many were against it.
- When Luther started writing hymns for the church in 1517, there was a great revolt.
- In 1540 Calvin stated that only the Old Testament Psalms

sung in a metrical rhythm were appropriate for worship (The Genevan Psalter). This caused great division in the church between Calvin's followers and Luther's.

- Near 1750 the Wesley brothers wrote hymns that taught theology and doctrine. It again caused great struggle among church leaders.

- The music of the 1880s Sunday School Era was looked down on by many because the hymns and testimony songs being written were subjective (personal) and not objective (directed toward God). Many thought there was no room for music like that in the church.

- Jazz influences of the early twentieth century brought out an edict from the Pope that the piano was forbidden in the Catholic church because of its worldly influences.

- Soon after came the Jesus Movement with drums, bass, guitars, and other instruments. Choruses and praise songs were following close behind, and all of it was hotly debated in the church.

- Over the years, there have been church and denominational splits, personal strife, and broken relationships, causing those in the church to quarrel bitterly and those outside the church to look at the church with contempt.

The list can go on and on, describing conflict over the years.

In recent decades, because of the potential for conflict in introducing people to music that differs from their current personal preferences, the church has just added another service to meet those preferential needs—thus the rise of the "contemporary service" in the last decades of the twentieth century until today. This has essentially prevented many churches from experiencing worship wars because, rather than challenging the status quo with change, another service is added, hopefully keeping everyone content. Only years later are the negative results beginning to show up in the churches, creating a desire to bring unity in worship throughout the local church.

As I have described, personal preferences are at the root of worship wars. The old expression fits well here: "We like what we know, and we know what we like." While personal tastes are not unimportant, neither are they what should drive our decisions.

Personal preferences are those things that make us feel at home, comfortable, and at ease. As much as we like to think of ourselves as totally objective, we all have a bias that favors our preferences. Proverbs 21:2a says, "Every way of a man is right in his own eyes." We tend to consider people with differing likes or viewpoints inferior or wrong. Extending that to worship, we tend to equate our preferences with God's preferences. Those that prefer singing from their hymnals while accompanied by a piano and organ may feel that churches that have worship led by a band, sing modern worship songs, have different lighting, and even architectural ideas are not what God desires.

Sadly, I see this even among church worship leaders. I was attending a conference a few years ago that had a more traditional worship inclination. I had a booth there to give out information about worship leadership training and other things our ministry offered. I was overhearing the teacher in an adjacent classroom who spoke with disdain and strong criticism of churches that prescribed to any of the modern worship practices. It was clear from the teacher's words that he felt it was an abomination!

James 4:1 states: "What causes quarrels and what causes fights among you? Is it not this, that your passions are at war within you?" **Our passions/personal preferences are the root of the conflict in worship style.** I will confront this as we continue through this material.

MISSIONARY MINDSET

As worship planners and leaders, we need to think like missionaries as we select songs, arrange music, etc. But just what does that mean?

In my worship leadership training events, I ask the people to imagine that we have gathered as a group of Christians from differing areas who desire to plant churches. In the first year of our organization, we choose a church in eastern Europe. I describe the country and the challenges for evangelism and church planting and then tell them what city we will be planting in. One of the churches from the United States represented in our group is growing significantly, and God is at work in a mighty way. Therefore, I suggest we plant a church just like that one—worship style and everything—in that city in eastern Europe. The participants in the training immediately say that it is not a good idea. I ask, "Why?" They say we must first study the culture to see how to connect with them. I then report on my findings from visiting the city and share a video of young people worshipping in that city. While our expectations would be a band with modern worship music, this large gathering of students was led by a choir, keyboard, and a stringed instrument. In fact, most worship settings around the city seemed to connect with multiple generations with this same basic style. We decide to plant a church based on this information. One year later, we discover the church is growing exponentially!

Now we gather to plant a second church. This one is in

the very rural section of a country in Africa. I comment that we have had great success from our European church, so in the spirit of duplicating what is successful, we should plant a cookie-cutter copy of that church in rural Africa. That always gets strong opposition from those attending the training event. They suggest dancing and rhythm would be appropriate. We discuss cultural differences between the two people groups. I then show a video from worship in that region, which is quite different from the European worship example. There is indeed much physical involvement and rhythmic accompaniment.

Then we discuss planting a third church. This one is located at your church's physical address. There comes a moment of revelation. Doesn't that make you think about what your church's worship should look like? Does our church's worship style reflect what a missionary may discover as the best way to reach the field God has for your church? If not, there are probably changes that will need to be made. We will discuss healthy ways to do that a bit later.

Ed Stetzer and Thom Rainer, in their book *Transformational Church* stated:

> *Leaders need to plan the worship service not in their heads but in their communities. Use the missionary mentality and discern the heart language of your community. Musical choices must be appropriate to the context.*[32]

We should not expect a missionary from our church to go to a tribe in Africa and ask them to worship with an organ and piano, singing Western hymns. Yet, we find nothing wrong with asking people in our communities (who may never encounter music of the type we use in our churches) to come and worship

God in forms that are very foreign to them. If we genuinely want to reach those who did not grow up in the church, we need to seek ways to speak a language they understand. The message never changes, nor is it watered down, but the delivery system of that message must stay relevant to reach people today.

> **Our worship should not be so foreign to our guests that they cannot understand it.
> How does this impact future decisions about corporate worship at your church?**

ESSENCE AND EXPRESSION OF WORSHIP

In his book, *The Church Awakening*, Chuck Swindoll uses two words to help us drill deeper into this discussion—*essence* and *expression*. He says that "the *essence* of worship has to do with our internalizing our adoration. It is a clear, definitive, conscious connection with the living God."[33]

So in the above examples of the church plants in Europe and Africa, we could say that the *essence* of their worship was the same. Their adoration, love, and passion for God could well be equal. It is nearly impossible for us to judge their hearts, but for the sake of this discussion, we can assume both groups were in love with God at an equal level.

Swindoll goes on to say that "the *expression* of worship moves us into the outward forms of worship … the ways we express our praise to God. That may be as varied as whatever culture is expressing it."[34]

The *expression* of worship between the European and African church plants was vastly different. It was related to the culture of the people there.

Swindoll notes that worship wars are when people clash over the *expression* of worship. I find this to be so true. I have never been working with a church in worship conflict where the problem is that people are criticized for loving Jesus more than others. It almost always involves worship expressions that draw heavily on personal preferences. What instruments do I utilize in worship? What styles of music? What physical involvement? What do worship leaders wear? The list goes on.

NONESSENTIALS AND ESSENTIALS OF WORSHIP

Another area where personal preferences can invade and create conflict in the church is that of nonessentials. It is vital for the church to consider everything they do carefully and determine if these practices (furnishings, attire, or whatever) are biblically mandated or just a cultural or preferential choice that entered the church sometime in the past.

What are some non-essentials? The pulpit. Choir robes. Piano. Organ. Band. Pews. Floor coverings. The list goes on and on. As you read these words, I am sure many of you immediately thought of conflict in a church in one or more of these areas.

Unfortunately, **non-essentials can be barriers to reaching our communities for Christ**. Let me give some examples I have encountered.

Illustration #1: I was working with a church seeking a healthy transition from two different styles of worship offered to one unified style. We met for several hours on a Saturday to work through a lot of the material you have in your hand today. The topic of the pulpit arose. One senior adult lady passionately spoke of the importance of the "sacred desk," with prominence and construction symbolizing the authority and centrality of the Word of God in our lives. She talked about how it was necessary for worship in their church. Her argument, in many ways, was compelling. I then asked a well-respected young lady what she thought of the pulpit. She talked of how the pulpit seemed to be a barrier between her and the pastor; when he preached from behind that large piece of furniture, there did not seem to be the connection she had when he was out from behind it. She commented that it was hard to explain, but the pulpit, she felt, hurt communication.

For the first time, the senior adult lady saw that her preference was actually a barrier to the gospel for others, and she was then willing to give it up. She realized that her preference was not based on scriptural requirements for worship and that the pulpit was not essential to worship. So often, just hearing other sides of issues makes a tremendous difference in achieving unity.

Illustration #2: One of our North Carolina Baptist churches had an unwritten dress code that you should dress in very nice clothes for worship, with dresses for ladies and suits for men. As they began to reach out to their neighborhood and invite people to come to be a part of worship on Sunday morning, they quickly discovered that the community often saw the "dress code" issue as a barrier to their attendance. People in the community did not have appropriate clothing to attend the church. Dressy clothing, the church discovered, can be a barrier to the gospel and has no biblical basis for being essential. Thus, many in the church determined that this unwritten dress code was a nonessential.

Later, I was telling this story to another church in conflict. One of the participants told me that their church, in past years, had a solution for the problem. If someone showed up at their church wearing non-compliant clothing, they ushered them to a clothing donation area to help them find something appropriate. I am sure that church was having trouble reaching their community!

Illustration #3: This is probably the saddest one of all. I had been leading worship training for people in a closed East Asian country for several days. On the last day, I had a question-and-answer session. One lady who was probably in her early 80s asked if her church could worship if they did not have a band. She was earnest. She had seen the rise of bands for worship and realized her church did not have musicians to lead that way. With tears in my eyes, I told this dear saint that when people in the United States asked me that question, I pointed them to her country where Christians had to worship in utter silence in secret for years. I told her their worship was probably greater than any worship in the world led by a full band with great singers. Once again, a feeling that something is essential, when there is no biblical basis for it, can cause unnecessary conflict in the church and hurt the church's missional approach.

Swindoll, in discussing essentials and nonessentials, says: "When nonessentials threaten unity, they should die."[35] Providing death for nonessentials is easier said than done. We will discuss ways to provide transition in a healthy manner later.

First Baptist Church of Durham, North Carolina spent considerable time looking at essentials and nonessentials in the area of worship. They designated the two areas as *timeless* (essentials) and *temporary* (nonessentials). They identified worship core values that they found in the Bible. This is what they said about how they will work with those areas deemed *timeless* and those that are *temporary*:

> *Two equal and opposite dangers face churches in every generation who are seeking to maintain healthy corporate worship: on the one hand, we are tempted to change what is timeless; on the other hand, we are tempted to refuse to change what is temporary.*
>
> *Godly leaders must be very clear on what is timeless in corporate worship—the Scripture, God, Christ, human sinfulness, the Gospel, and the like. Godly leaders must also recognize that every generation and every culture has its heart in language which enables its people to worship with passion, and that that heart language is constantly evolving in its outward forms.*
>
> *To change the timeless matters of the Christian faith is to betray the gospel itself and become reeds swayed by the wind of public opinion. To cling to temporary forms when their time is done is to become stubborn traditionalists whose local churches will soon become obsolete—old inflexible wineskins which rupture with the new wine of the Spirit.*
>
> *One single force drives church leaders in each of these opposite dangers: fear of man. The remedy is to derive clarity from Scripture and courage from the Spirit to stand firm on what is timeless and lovingly change in due time what must change.*[36]

> **What are some non-essentials of worship?**
> **What specific examples have you seen**
> **that cause conflict in your church?**

UNIFIED WORSHIP

Much of what I have been discussing in this book leads us to the concept of *unified* worship. It is not contemporary worship. It is not traditional worship. It is not really *blended* worship as many experience it—you know, when one-half of your songs are traditional songs and one-half are modern songs, and you end up making people mad half the time! I see this blended experience so often in churches. When you sing a hymn, many people in the congregation seem to disconnect while others are singing out and involved. Then, when you sing a modern worship song, many people fold their arms and just stare with distaste, anxiously waiting to get done with the song. Others, at the same time, are singing passionately with great expression. THIS IS NOT UNIFIED WORSHIP. This is worship with great division by preferences without any sacrifice for unity offered.

To look at an order of worship, you will not be able to tell for sure if the church experiences unity in worship. Achieving this goal is far more than programmatic artistry. Let's dig deeper.

In Swindoll's book, he rightly notes:

> *Christians' love for one another should be preeminent. Christian unity and genuine worship can only occur in a context of **love**.*[37]

This is a crucial component of unified worship. There must be love between the people in the congregation. **Without love, there will be no sacrifice. Without love, there will be no unity.** Swindoll goes on to say:

> *When self-centered desires reign supreme, there will never be unity in the body of Christ, much less in worship. But when self-sacrifice is the priority, unity falls into place.*[38]

Discuss Swindoll's quote about *self-centered* versus *self-sacrifice* in relation to your church's corporate worship.

This concept is vital to understanding unified worship. *Self-sacrifice* and *love* are keys to achieving this biblical ideal. Let me illustrate a church experiencing unified worship.

Imagine you are visiting a church that you have not attended before. As you enter the sanctuary, you see that it is a fan-shaped room. Canned music is playing, and the church is abuzz with conversations as people arrive from their homes or Bible study classes. You notice that people of all generations gather—young children, great-grandmas, middle-aged couples, college students, teenagers—a healthy mix of ages. You are greeted warmly by a lady at the door and are offered help in finding a seat. You thank her and go in on your own.

A band on stage gets into their places to be ready when the countdown hits zero. There is an air of anticipation and excitement. You sit in the center section near the middle. As you move to your seat, you notice an older teen sitting a couple of rows up on the right. He looks different from most others—obviously connected to a subculture you cannot identify. He is talking with a middle-aged couple in front of him, and they seem to know each other. He appears to have a friend with him as well. You turn to the left and see, on the same row, an elderly lady sitting by herself. She has a radiance of joy about her. You wonder what she is doing in a church that seems this "modern" in its worship approach.

Before I continue the story, let me reveal some backstories. The teenager's name is Brad. Someone from this church invited him a couple of years ago as he sought what to do with his life. He came and kept coming back for more. Soon he gave his life to Jesus and began to study His Word daily with great interest. He soon began sharing Christ with his friends and bringing them to church. He has become involved in much of the life of the church in the last year, getting to know people of all ages.

The elderly lady is affectionately known as "Sister Mable." She and her husband were two of the original people who planted this church over 40 years ago with a desire to see the church as a lighthouse to the community. She loves her church, and she loves that it is still reaching the community so well. They experience baptisms every month. The church worship style has changed quite a bit since the early years when they sang from the hymnal with an organ and piano.

Let's get back to the story. This morning the service opens with a high-powered praise song. The band is really engaged. Brad is very much into worship, not only singing with all his might but also physically demonstrative in his worship. This song is not one of Sister Mable's favorite styles of songs. She is not necessarily fond of those electric guitars being so strong. However, as she sees Brad worshipping to her right, she is reminded of how she has prayed for years for this church to remain a lighthouse to the community and is so thankful to see people like Brad coming to Christ and worshipping Him with all their being. Out of her love, she begins to really sing the song, and within a little time, she is passionately singing the words and genuinely worshipping her Savior.

A bit later in the service, the band takes on more of an acoustic flavor, and they lead the hymn, *The Old Rugged Cross*. Sister Mable sings this old favorite and begins to recall a time in her and her late husband's lives when God delivered them that connects with this song. She begins to weep and sing with lots of emotion. Now Brad feels the words and music of this song are somewhat archaic, and they don't fit in his musical preference; yet he sees how Mable is moved by the song and engaged in worship. Mable has spent much time in the last months talking to Brad and seems to really love him. He begins to sing the song out of his love and respect for her. When he gets to the chorus, he is singing for all he is worth, "I'll cherish the old rugged cross."

You see, **there is a mutual sacrifice of personal preferences for the unity of the body.** Brad and Mable are willing to defer their personal preferences and participate in these otherwise less desirable songs because of their love and respect for each other. **I believe as they make this sacrifice for the unity of the body, the Spirit truly helps them to worship wholly with these songs.**

As this happens, true unity in worship takes place.

C.S. Lewis said:

> *I dislike very much their hymns, which I considered to be fifth-rate poems set to sixth-rate music. But as I went on I saw the great merit of it. ... I realized that the hymns were, nevertheless, being sung with devotion and benefit by an old saint in elastic-side boots in the opposite pew, and then you realize that you aren't fit to clean those boots. It gets you out of your solitary conceit.*[39]

It is a mutual sacrifice of personal preferences for the unity of the body.

Jesus prayed "that they may all be one, just as you, Father, are in me, and I in you, that they also may be in us, so that the world may believe that you have sent me." John 17:21

This prayer for the church indicated Christ's desire for us to be ONE in our worship so that the world may believe in Him. Think about it. In this world of having it your way—the television programs you choose, the way your hamburger is prepared, the options on your new car, etc.—for someone to enter a sanctuary and see multiple generations and ethnicities with different preferences actually worshipping together in unity, **that shows the power of the gospel to confound the wisdom of the world, to bring together diverse people in unity.**

I was working with a group of church leaders seeking to move from two different styles of worship to a unified style. When we were discussing the mutual sacrifice of personal preferences, one senior adult lady spoke up and said, "I am willing to make whatever sacrifices are needed to find unity in worship ... as long as the younger generation makes as many sacrifices as we do!" I could hardly believe what I had heard and was preparing a response for her in my head. Before I could say anything, another senior lady spoke up and said, "In my long life with Jesus as my Savior and Lord, I have made many sacrifices, and every time I have made a sacrifice, I have found complete joy and contentment." Enough said.

Many of our churches practice ageism. They divide the congregations into separate worshipping groups giving each their preference in music. Yes, there are some significant reasons for separating the church into different venues; however, we must also consider the biblical teaching:

> *Do not rebuke an older man but encourage him as you would a father, younger men as brothers, older women as mothers, younger women as sisters, in all purity.* 1 Timothy 5:1-3
>
> *Let no one despise you for your youth, but set the believers an example in speech, in conduct, in love, in faith, in purity.* 1 Timothy 4:12
>
> *One generation shall commend your works to another, and shall declare your mighty acts.* Psalm 145:4

What are some barriers to achieving unity in worship? How can your church work together to overcome those barriers?

As you can see, the song selection does not dictate whether or not the service would be classified as *unified* or *blended*. It is much more a matter of the heart, an attitude of love and self-sacrifice, that in the giving, we truly can worship in other forms than our preferences would dictate. Now I will attempt a succinct description of unified worship:

> *People across generations, ethnicities, and/or cultures often hold different preferences.* **Unified worship** *is achieved when they worship God together, laying aside preferences through the transformational power of the gospel. In unity, genuine worship takes place.*

If you noticed, in the story I shared, there was a connection between Brad and Sister Mable. It is hard to develop bonds of love between people with whom you have no relationship. So as church leaders who want to establish unity in worship (as well as the entirety of the church), we need to think about how we facilitate love and self-sacrifice among the people. You must invite your people to do life together in various ways, such as:

- a mission project intentionally putting young and old side by side working together
- senior adults "adopting" a young person to spend time with, pray for, etc.
- times of fellowship and fun with intergenerational groupings
- small groups of varying ages studying a book of the Bible or a topic
- ministry teams with young and old serving together as greeters, tech team, or worship team, etc.
- creation of prayer partners linking young and old
- creation of an intergenerational choir, with participants sitting with people of another generation
- any activity or ministry project that puts together young and old

You get the idea. **Having young and old do life together will result in getting to know each other while breaking down generational barriers. As a result, they begin to love and respect one another and are more willing to give up their personal preferences for others.**

Tullian Tchividjian, in his book *Unfashionable* writes:

> Many churches offer a "traditional service" for the tribe who prefers old music and a "contemporary service" for the tribe who prefers new music. I understand the good intentions behind some of these efforts but something as seemingly harmless as this evidences a fundamental failure to comprehend the heart of the Gospel.
>
> When we offer, for instance, a contemporary worship service for the younger people and a traditional worship service for the older people, we are not only feeding tribalism (which is a toxic form of racism) but we are saying that the Gospel can't successfully bring these two different groups together.
>
> It is a declaration of doubt in the reconciling power of God's Gospel. Generational appeal in worship is an unintentional admission that the Gospel is powerless to "join together" what man has separated.[40]

I discovered a post by Jim Bradford, Ph.D., the senior pastor of Central Assembly of God in Springfield, Missouri, where he speaks to this idea:

> When we experience times of tension, I may say to the seniors, "I probably cannot give you all you want in a primary service—hymns and older choruses from beginning to end. The worship service may not completely satisfy you, but don't you want a church where your kids and grandkids want to come and worship?"

In this way I talk to seniors about worship in a language they understand. Seniors want their children and grandchildren—the younger generation—to enjoy coming to their church and worshipping the Lord. So I ask them for tolerance, encouraging them to grow with us in this. At Central Assembly, we have a large number of senior adults, so we have hymn-sing nights and encourage the singing of hymns in our Sunday School classes.

But if music is a language for each generation, we cannot build a church using only one language. When I talk to the younger generation, I tell them we need the hymns. I might do a message where I intertwine [music] with the preaching of the Word. I will illustrate with hymns or talk about the Scripture behind certain hymns, and then sing them. But more importantly, I instruct them and walk them through what worship really is.

We need to have our own kind of worship. We need to be able to worship in our own musical language. But we also need tolerance, living with generosity toward one another. In my opinion, the older generations have a greater responsibility to defer to the younger generation than vice versa. As those who are more mature, they should be quicker to default to the needs of the younger, much like a parent to the child.[41]

I like where he points out that those who are more mature should be quicker to default to the needs of the younger ones. Not only does this make sense along the lines of spiritual maturity, but also in allowing change that is needed as the church moves into the future.

LEADING HEALTHY CHANGE IN WORSHIP

Ultimately, change in worship should come only after seeking God's heart to determine needed adjustments. Some leaders instigate change for the wrong reasons, such as emulating a thriving church across town or one they have seen on the internet, wanting to be cutting edge in their approach, or chasing after their own personal preferences. Change must be a result of God's direction.

> **Have you seen churches encounter bad experiences as they navigated worship change? Why do you think the changes were not going well?**

WHY CHANGE?

Why would a church need to change its worship? As I mentioned in the introduction, some churches are stuck to old forms of worship that no longer connect with the people, and the churches are dying; worship has become rote and lifeless. I was spending time with a missionary in one region of our state that worked with around 50 churches. He shared with me that he thought as many as 30 would be closing their doors in the next ten years because of a lack of relevance and no desire to make changes. Some churches fail to communicate in a language of today; video is perhaps the greatest tool for communication, yet some churches still resist adding screens. Why would we not want to use the powerful medium of video to share the greatest story ever told and to connect powerfully with the congregants in worship? Some churches are not taking on a missionary mindset regarding their worship.

Many churches I encounter want to stay the same. They are comfortable doing things in the way they have always done them. In the book, *Flickering Lamps: Christ and His Church*, Henry and Richard Blackaby write:

> One of the great deceptions many dying churches believe is that they don't need to make any significant changes; they just need a pastor to help them continue doing what they have always done.[42]

Indeed, worship change is needed in most churches I have encountered, but how do we make those changes in an appropriate manner?

WHY IS THERE CONFLICT IN CHANGE?

Unfortunately, church leaders often instigate change in very unhealthy manners, bringing about great division. Changing too fast can be a great cause for conflict in the church. We often want change, and we want it now; yet a wiser approach moves more slowly, gaining buy-in and helping people understand the reasons behind the change. Failing to help people understand the reasons for the change and not gaining support can cause great dissension.

Chuck Lawless of Southeastern Baptist Theological Seminary lists several mistakes leaders make in transitioning a church's worship[43]:

1. **Poor communication with church members.** I'm convinced many more church members will get on board if they understand the *why* behind changes. When we give only the *what* without the *why*, our folks will likely lack the motivation to change.

2. **Inadequate responses to resistant people.** People who are resistant aren't necessarily bad people. Sometimes, frankly, their input would have saved us from trouble. Simply hearing their concerns can go a long way toward gaining their support.

3. **Too much too soon.** Leaders who want "microwave" change often run over people who still prefer the stove. The microwave may be much more effective, but the wise leader knows he must discover the right pace to move in that direction.

4. **Overdependence on methodologies.** Methodologies are not insignificant. In fact, good missiology leads us to ask about the most appropriate method for a given context. Methodologies, though, are never answers in themselves. Constant methodological changes without sensitivity for people can wear out the church.

5. **Borrowing vision.** It's good to learn from other churches, and the internet gives us more opportunity than ever to do so. If we only copy other churches, though, we risk reducing our congregation to a project. Every church is different, and everyone should seek God's vision.

6. **Short-term commitment.** The pastor who wants to lead a

church through change toward growth must be committed to stay there awhile. Indeed, the pastor with a short-term commitment will likely have only a short-term vision.

7. **Mirrorless leadership.** Some leaders of transitioning churches use a magnifying glass to see faults in their church, but they use no mirror to see their own deficiencies. Their tendency to blame the congregation for all the problems makes the transition that much more difficult.

8. **Reactive praying.** The tendency of many churches working through change is to make decisions and implement plans – and *then* ask God to bless those plans. We shouldn't be surprised if our plans don't work if we don't seek God's guidance until after we've implemented them.

9. **Loveless shepherding.** I wish we saw no need to add this mistake, but we've seen it too much to ignore it. Many leaders want to change a church they've never grown to love, and that lack of affection makes it easier to "run over" the people who appear to be in the way.

10. **Giving up too easily.** Moving a congregation is seldom easy. It often takes more energy and more time than we had assumed. Leaders who leave early while blaming others may well miss what God has in store.

WORSHIP RENEWAL: A SPIRITUAL BATTLE

Perhaps the bottom line on conflict around worship in the church is the fact that Satan desires to divide a church in the very area where it gains its power and fuel for effectiveness in all other spheres of ministry—worship. If Satan can create a sense of satisfaction with meaningless worship and cause conflict with the process of changing to something that engages your people and community to encounter God, he will undoubtedly do so. **We need to recognize that worship renewal/worship change is a very real spiritual battle where we need to wage war against the enemy.**

HOW DO WE GET TO THE DESIRED FUTURE?

Once we have a clear vision from God as to the direction our times of gathered worship should take, how do we get there in a healthy, God-honoring, people-loving manner with biblical and musical excellence?

First, you need to realize that just changing the gathered worship in a church is not the key to spiritual renewal and worship revitalization. There must first be spiritual change.

Graham Kendrick has a powerful statement about this:

> *It is impossible to draw rich worship from poverty-stricken hearts. Worship should develop alongside spiritual growth, ... but if we merely impose new styles and methods on top of a dead situation, we will end up with nothing better than a beautifully decorated coffin.*[44]

Unified worship can never be achieved in a congregation that lacks spiritual maturity. There becomes too much of a seeking one's own agenda over the unity of the body.

As Swindoll says, "When self-centered desires reign supreme, there will never be unity in the body of Christ, much less in worship. But when self-sacrifice is the priority, unity falls into place."[45]

A powerful example of this was seen in a church I worked with a few years ago. The church had two services of differing styles. They were experiencing much division in their church and made it clear, more than anything, they wanted to come back together in worship—to be one in worship once again. Much work was done in the process, but the conflict was coming to a head. Unity could not be attained. The problem was that the people said they wanted unity in worship, but actually, they wanted everyone to come together in the style of worship they preferred. The traditional worship people wanted the contemporary worship people to join them in singing hymns with an organ and a piano, and the contemporary worship people wanted the traditional people to come to their band-led service. There was no willingness for a mutual sacrifice of personal preferences for the unity of the body, nor was love pervasive in the attempt to come together in unity.

STEPS TO A HEALTHY TRANSITION

In working with and observing several churches going through worship change, I have determined several steps to moving in a healthy manner:

Spiritual preparation. As I mentioned earlier, spiritual renewal is a prerequisite to worship change. If people are cold-hearted in their worship, just changing things will do no good. Spend time helping your church seek God in their lives and revitalize. I have seen some churches have weeks of focused time for renewal with prayer efforts, small groups, daily devotions, and more, helping people find personal renewal.

Prayer. Obviously, prayer is a part of spiritual renewal, but more than that, prayer needs to precede change, accompany change, and continue after the change. Remember that Satan wants to divide the church where it gets its power—corporate worship. Engage some of your prayer warriors to lift this up daily. Keep this in front of your people as you offer prayer needs for the church.

A loving heart. We need to have a loving heart for our people in times of change. Offer them hope. Help them see the desired future. Part of having a loving heart is to "do life" with your people—spend time with them in fellowship, small groups, mission projects, and other ways you can get to know them, and they get to know you. The more people know you and trust you, the more they will trust you in making changes in areas of worship. Discipling relationships are perhaps the best for getting to know someone on a spiritual level.

Another way to have a loving heart is to consider the difference between *demolition* and *deconstruction* when it comes to worship change. My friend, David Manner, explains it this way:

> *Demolition is the most expedient method of tearing down an existing structure in order to ensure that the ensuing structure bears no characteristics of the original structure.*
>
> *Does this sound like worship change in your congregation?*
>
> *In an effort to initiate worship change, leaders often use the finesse of a wrecking ball to swing wildly at existing practices. The consequence is often the complete destruction of the relational foundations of a community that may have taken decades to build.*
>
> *Deconstruction is the systematic and selective process of taking a structure apart while carefully preserving valuable elements for reuse. Deconstruction focuses on giving those materials within*

an existing structure a new life once it is determined that the existing structure will require change to continue functioning successfully.

Deconstruction is the realization that many of the components within an existing structure still have value. Healthier worship change is taking the time to recognize those components and harvest them in order to reclaim their value for useful building materials in the new structure.

Worship demolition causes destruction and requires invention. Worship deconstruction allows for renovation and encourages innovation. Both processes agree that worship transition is necessary as a congregation considers its culture and context. But worship deconstruction at least offers hope of a foundation on which to rebuild.[46]

I see examples of worship demolition often in churches. Here is one example: One church had a fantastic choir and orchestra full of highly talented people. A new pastor determined that the church needed to move to worship led by a band and vocal team and permanently dismissed the choir and orchestra. Now over 100 people gifted and called by God to use their musical talents in worship are told they are not needed. If a deconstruction strategy were employed, the choir could be repurposed as a worship-leading choir (which can be a huge catalyst for worship renewal), and the orchestra could be repurposed in how they are used as additions to rhythm section-led times of worship. Rather than being thrown out completely, the organ can be repurposed on more modern worship songs to play filler sounds, essentially as pads from a keyboard. In deconstruction, people are still loved and valued for their part in the body, and they can continue living out their calling to serve and honor God. **When possible,**

worship deconstruction can undoubtedly be the best path for unity in worship change. Look at those whom God has brought together in your church and utilize those gifts even if it doesn't fit the textbook model for your worship ministry. Every church has its own DNA for worship.

Cast vision. Leaders need to educate the people about the reasons for change and the processes being employed. Not only should this be done on the front end, but it needs to be a continual part of the time of change. So often, leaders talk about the need and the process frequently in their meetings and conversations. Still, the average church member may not be reminded of these things beyond the initial presentation. It is easy for them to forget about them. Write about it in newsletters, talk about it in worship services, and remind people about it in meetings and informal conversations. Keep it front of mind in everyone's lives. **The *why* is of utmost importance and needs to be communicated frequently.**

Leaders should present the biblical, cultural and missional understanding of worship to the congregation and let them wrestle with essentials and non-essentials in worship, as well as the concept of unified, intergenerational, multi-ethnic worship. In my experience, when people see what should be in worship and lay that beside the reality of worship in their own church and personal lives, the Holy Spirit begins to work in their lives to bring alignment.

Make change with transparency. When people know the *why* and understand the steps you are taking, they are more likely to trek along with you and not push back. In addition to casting the vision of the *why*, leaders need to continually help people understand the steps they are taking to reach the desired outcome.

Strive. Too often, leaders push forward only to shrink back due to criticism and other pushback. In striving, we must move toward the God-given goal without apologizing or pulling back. This does not mean to steamroller over people in the way. Obstacles must be dealt with lovingly (see Lawless' article above). However, we need to be persistent in our pursuit of the goal.

I turn again to a blog post by my friend David Manner who illustrates the importance of this:

> *The legend is told that when Alexander the Great and his men arrived on the shores of Persia they encountered an enemy that drastically outnumbered them. Since it was clear that the odds were against them and the future was uncertain, his men pleaded with Alexander to retreat to the boats and the safety of their homeland to regroup and get more men.*
>
> *Alexander was so certain that their course of action was the correct one that he ordered his men to burn their boats.*
>
> *As their only means of retreat went up in flames Alexander turned to his men and said, "We go home in Persian ships, or we die."*
>
> *If your congregation has determined that initiating change is necessary for you to retain those people you already have and gain those you don't have yet ... then conversely, failing to initiate change when change is necessary will kill your congregation. The death is usually a slow one ... but still terminal.*
>
> *Conviction and collaboration are the unifying factors that inspire leaders and congregants to refuse to retreat, go all in, and burn their boats even when the implementation of needed change is often frightening and the end result is rarely certain.*
>
> *Earnie Larson is credited with saying, "Nothing changes if*

nothing changes, and if I keep doing what I've always done, I'll keep getting what I've always got, and will keep feeling what I always felt."[47]

In summary, as you seek the direction you are to go in renewing the times of corporate worship in your church, lead your church in a time of spiritual renewal for all to come together seeking the face of God. Mobilize your prayer warriors, as well as the entire congregation, to be in prayer for the effort. Love your people unconditionally as you do life with them and minister with them. As you consider changes, find ways to use deconstruction rather than demolition. Keep the vision before the people continually—not only the *why* but also the *how*. Then remember, when you feel like taking two steps back after taking a step forward, think of Alexander, who would not allow his men to retreat. Don't look back. Press forward. Give God praise!

What are your biggest takeaways from this section that will help you navigate change in the worship ministry?

Understanding Worship Leadership

In the last chapter, we got a better idea of what worship is and dealt with many of the elemental concepts we need to grasp as worship leaders. Now, building on the foundations of chapter one, we will begin to work through some basic understandings of what it means to be a worship leader—the responsibilities of leading a congregation in worship that God has entrusted to you. Perhaps the best place to start is by understanding that God calls us to this leadership role. It is a high calling and one with great responsibility. To many, the concept of *calling* often seems very mysterious and not well understood.

A CALLING TO WORSHIP LEADING

As worship leaders, it is important for us to identify God's calling on our lives to the worship ministry. So let's take a bit of time to understand God's different calls on our lives. Much of the material I will be sharing with you comes from a most excellent book on understanding God's call, *Is God Calling Me?*[48] by Jeff Iorg. I highly recommend you read the book to grasp this subject much better. I will give you a brief overview here.

THREE TYPES OF CALL EXPERIENCES

There are three areas of calling that Christians may receive in their lives. All Christians will receive one call; others will receive three types of calls.

1. A universal call to Christian service

God calls every Christian to live a life for God's glory, to make disciples, to serve others, and to grow to become more like Christ every day. Every Christ-follower has been issued this call. There are numerous passages in the Bible to illustrate this calling. Ephesians 4:1-3 is one example:

> *I therefore, a prisoner for the Lord, urge you to walk in a manner worthy of the calling to which you have been called, with all humility and gentleness, with patience, bearing with one another in love, eager to maintain the unity of the Spirit in the bond of peace.*

Iorg talks about a tension that often comes up here:

> *So, what is the relationship of God's universal call to Christian service and a believer's vocation? God calls every believer in Christian service. God's universal call to Christian service can be expressed through any honest vocation. God wants and needs Christian teachers, plumbers, attorneys, mechanics, nurses, and carpenters. There is, however, a distinct call to ministry leadership that often (though not always) results in employment in a ministry position.[49]*

2. A general call to ministry leadership

The *distinct call* that Iorg mentions above, is described as a *general call* to *ministry leadership.* God calls some men and women to a specific ministry leadership role or responsibility, such as preaching, teaching, administration, pastoring, evangelism, worship ministry, and others. These positions may be full-time or part-time positions, paid or unpaid. The difference between the general call and the universal call to Christian service is the leadership part. *Some* people are called to be Christian leaders, while *all* are called to Christian service. The calling of the disciples gives some examples of this type of calling in the Bible.

God calls worship leaders in a general call to ministry leadership. The call confirms God's purpose for us and the gifts He has given us. It is not enough to know that God calls us to a specific leadership role; we must also understand more specifically *how* and *where* we are to utilize that role.

3. A specific call to a ministry assignment

For those called to ministry leadership, this type of call will come to a *specific assignment* that the person is to take. For instance, God may call you to worship leadership in your general call, but at some point, He will call you to a *specific* ministry position. This is where the struggle comes of what church or ministry organization to serve, when to move from one church or organization to another, and what exactly your ministry position is (worship, missions and worship, worship and senior adults, etc.). God has a plan for you in this, and we are to seek Him to determine our calling to a specific ministry assignment. We can see examples of God's calling/leading to particular assignments throughout the New Testament, especially in the book of Acts.

God calls all Christians to the *universal call of Christian service* and some Christians to the *general call of ministry leadership*; and those He calls to ministry leadership also receive a *specific call to a ministry assignment.*

THREE WAYS GOD CALLS

If you talk to ministry leaders, you will discover that the realization of God's call, both the general and the specific calls, on one's life can come in a variety of ways. Through talking with others and exploring the biblical texts, we see there are three primary ways that God calls ministry leaders. Again, I will outline the three ways that Iorg brings out in his book.

1. Sudden experiences

God calls through sudden, even dramatic experiences, as is greatly illustrated in Saul's Damascus road conversion or Moses' burning bush experience. Sometimes God may use a crisis in your life to get your attention and help you discover His call on your life. Perhaps God uses other circumstances to conform you to His will. Dramatic calling is powerful but is not common. Do not feel slighted or less called if your calling was not a sudden experience.

My calling to leave the local church ministry that I loved and move to denominational service was much of a *sudden experience* in my life. I had been serving as the missions and worship pastor of a church for 23 years at the time. One day I spoke to God in my time of solitude in personal worship and basically said, "God, I love it here and could easily spend the rest of my life serving you in this place, but if there is anything else you want me to do with my life, please let me know." Within 24 hours one unbelievable thing happened after another. These things could not be explained away as coincidences. After a couple of weeks of jaw-dropping occurrences, I was 100% confident that God was calling me to the work as a worship consultant for North Carolina Baptists. I might add, that having that confirmation in my calling is a great help on weeks when I get discouraged and may want to throw in the towel. In those moments, God reminds me that He absolutely called me to this place and has not called me away. I can serve with renewed zeal, just remembering His definite calling on my life.

2. Reasoned decisions

As you are seeking God's will for your general or specific call, sometimes that involves reasoning through various decisions as you lean upon God in prayer and Bible study. Often these callings may take place over a long period of time.

The call to my first church after graduating from seminary was one of *reasoned decisions*. I had three interested churches set up interviews with me in a single week. My wife and I prayed for God to make His call clear if one of these was where we were to invest our lives and ministry. We talked with the three pastors and the search teams at length. I considered how the pastors and churches aligned with my convictions and worship ideals. As we prayed and reasoned, we felt a conviction, a drawing, and excitement all around the church in Statesville, North Carolina. We felt beyond doubt that it was the place to align ourselves. Time after time, God confirmed that call in the next 23 years of serving there.

3. Prompting of others

At times, God will send a messenger or a number of messengers to relay His truth to you. It may be a mentor, a friend, or even someone you do not know. The call of Barnabas and Saul to missionary work in Acts 13 came in this way. God can indeed use His children to relay messages.

A worship leader friend of mine, Daniel Byers, shared with me a remarkable story of this type of calling in his life. While attending a three-day spiritual renewal and formation retreat, "Walk to Emmaus," a guy whom Daniel had never encountered before came up to him and told him he had a message from God. Daniel was a bit amused by this and asked him what the message God wanted to relay was. The man said, "You are going to be a minister." Daniel relays:

> Not trying to be rude I laughed shortly in the guy's face. I told him, "Okay, thanks," and walked away. Now growing up as a preacher's kid there were so many times when I knew the Lord was calling me into ministry but refused because of watching the struggle of ministry in my dad's life. My father has served in various roles in many churches--worship pastor, youth pastor, and senior pastor. I know how hard being called into ministry can be.
>
> About two years later, a service tech came to our home; I had never seen the man before. After completing the repair, he asked me if I believed in Jesus Christ. I told him I do. In return, he said, "God has a message for you." In shock, knowing what he was about to say, I asked him to tell me the message. He told me that I would soon become a minister. I once again laughed and said, "Okay, thank you." Then the man left, and I have never seen him again.

The senior pastor in the church that Daniel attended had been asking him to move into a worship leadership role there since their worship pastor had recently left the church. Despite the two strangers giving Daniel a word from God that he was to go into the ministry, Daniel replied that he needed a drastic call, a Moses' experience, to say "yes" to this ministry opportunity.

Later that year, while visiting his parents, Daniel's family attended worship one Sunday morning at the church where his dad pastored. The message was from Psalm 100:1-5. Daniel commented:

> *That morning as my father preached, I had my Moses experience. God spoke to me in a way like never before. Without a doubt, I knew it was Him. I felt like I was the only person in the room, and it was clear that He was calling me into ministry. God used two complete strangers in my life to bring a message that He was calling me into ministry.*

Daniel submitted to the call of God on His life and indicates it has been one of the best decisions he has ever made. While the prompting of others is more often from people you know, God can use complete strangers to relay His calling to you.

DISCERNING GOD'S CALL

Iorg mentions a few ways that Christians can discern God's call. The Holy Spirit gives you an inner peace about the decision; you receive confirmation from others that your decision seems right; as you evaluate your effectiveness in ministry, you realize you are equipped for the calling; and you find joy in serving God through that ministry. Often, people are afraid to follow the call of God in their lives because they believe they will have to give up things that bring joy to their lives. They often just see sacrifice. When you align yourself with God's calling in your life, you will find the greatest joy possible. That does not mean life will be easy and without hardships, but it does mean that God is with you through it all, and you will find great joy, fulfillment, and purpose in life.

GOD'S USE OF A COMBINATION OF WAYS TO REVEAL HIS CALL

Even though I have presented three ways God calls, I must point out that sometimes God will use two or three of these ways to make His call clear to people.

I was one of those stubborn people who needed a full-court press to get my attention about my career choice. My call to worship leadership was just that. I entered college feeling confident that I could best serve God as a physician. I loved science and math with a passion and was greatly loving the pre-med curriculum at UNC-Chapel Hill. Then God got my attention with a *sudden, drastic call experience*—my mom's cancer. That shook up my world. In addition, I was placed in leadership positions in our Baptist Campus Ministry in worship and music, including being tasked to lead a choir. This was nowhere on my radar nor in my wheelhouse. I kept being asked to take on other ministry leadership roles. Then there came several people close to me who asked if I had considered that God might be calling me to ministry—*this was the prompting of others*. I finally began to give in to the idea that this might be something God was doing in my life. I began to seek the counsel of mature Christians, including my campus ministers, my pastor, people at the Baptist State Convention of North Carolina I had come to know, and friends who knew me well. I spent time reading about the will of God, praying, searching the Bible for answers, and more. For nearly a year I went through *reasoned decisions* as I sought answers. Eventually, I switched my major to music and began my trek to pursue the education I needed for my new calling in life. The process brought me much closer to God and gave me renewed purpose and a passion for my calling.

Your story will be unique to you. Just recognize that God uses many ways to help us discern His call. I am reminded of a life-changing study I experienced entitled, *Experiencing God*, by Henry Blackaby and Claude King. In that study, the authors write that "God speaks by the Holy Spirit through the Bible, prayer, circumstances, and the church, to reveal Himself, His purposes, and His ways."[50] I believe this is spot on with the ways God calls. When you are seeking His calling, pour yourself into Bible study and prayer, asking God to reveal His will. Talk with mature Christians (the church) and look at the circumstances God has used in your life to prepare you for your calling.

> **Take some time to reflect on your own life and calling. Do you feel confident that God has called you to worship leadership? Are you struggling to determine if He is calling? Are you reasonably sure He is calling, but you continue to ignore the call?**

A MAJOR, PIVOTAL TIME IN MY LIFE RELATED TO CALLING AND PASSION

Before we move on, I want to share this additional calling experience because it has shaped so much of my life as a worship leader, consultant, and teacher. Not only will this illustrate my wrestling with calling, but it will help you understand many of the perspectives of the remainder of this book. **Please don't**

skip over this session, because I believe my learnings are foundational to the rest of this book.

Later in my ministry, four churches contacted me in two days, asking me to consider serving their churches as their worship pastor. This got my attention because I had not submitted my resume anywhere as someone interested in moving. It was not a consideration in my mind to leave the church I was serving. However, I could not overlook the fact that four churches contacted me in two days. Within a week, a few other churches also reached out. Something was up. I felt God was indeed trying to get my attention.

As I struggled through seeking God's will in the matter of what church God wanted me to be in, I was able to narrow the choices down to five – two in North Carolina, one in South Carolina, one in Texas, and the church I currently served (with the thought that perhaps God was not calling me away). That same week, I received a brochure on a worship conference at another church in the same area of Texas as the church that had contacted me. I had previously sensed a need for a time of retreat and renewal in the area of worship. I was also interested in making an unannounced visit to the Texas church that had reached out to me. Little did I know that my time in Texas would have such an impact on my life as a worship leader.

My great friend, Tim Stutts (then serving as interim youth pastor of the church I served), and I went to the conference. On Sunday morning, we attended the Texas church that had contacted me. They were running over 2,000 total in three worship services—two blended and one contemporary. We decided to attend both styles. The church was fast growing and outwardly looked very healthy. What God showed me that day surprised me. I believe He was using this time to do something in my life but was not sure what.

The blended service was a great "production," with every part of the service well-rehearsed and the pastor well-polished. Somehow, it seemed fake. By the book, everything was done right, but there seemed to be an important element missing– God. I couldn't quite put my finger on it. The contemporary service spoke clearly. The place was packed out to capacity (around 1,000 people), and the well-prepared worship band and singers were doing it all by the book with the latest, greatest modern worship songs, blended together well in sets. Yet there was a MAJOR problem. I felt almost sick to my stomach as I looked around and saw what God was seeing. The people on stage were performing–like a rock concert, and the congregation (audience) was standing and seemingly having a good time, but not participating in any tangible way. Almost no one was singing. No one seemed connected at all to worship. It was a mass of spectators. Later that day, God led me to Revelation 2 and 3. First, the account of the Church in Ephesus that was busy with God's work, but they had forsaken their first love, and second, the story of the Church in Sardis that had a reputation of being alive but was dead. God showed me that this church was indeed BUSY growing and offering programs–it indeed looked like a thriving, healthy church. Yet God showed me that morning His view of a church that does not worship. I began to examine my own heart and the worship life back home at the church I served. *Were we any different from this church?*

That Sunday night, Tim and I attended the opening session of the worship conference. It was a worship service involving their choir and congregation with conference participants being a part of the congregation. I cannot begin to express to you the difference between the two churches. This was truly a church where the glory of God dwells. The service was Spirit-filled, and I believe almost everyone in attendance truly encountered God. I found myself caught up in heartfelt praise and worship, so much so that the "processing" side of me (which looks critically at worship services and music) shut down, and I was transported to God's presence. I sensed God saying to me, **"This is what I want you to be about in leading worship."** The conference was awesome from beginning to end. I had never attended a worship conference prior to this that was not about *form* but about *heart*. God began to birth in my heart a desire to be in His presence in worship and to authentically lead a congregation to that place.

There was great freedom of worship at that church. People felt the liberty to raise their hands in worship if they desired; but I sensed that those that did not feel comfortable worshipping that way felt fully accepted and involved. People had the freedom in worship to respond to God by going to the altar to pray whenever the Holy Spirit began working on them; they did not have to quench the Spirit and wait for an "acceptable" time at the end of the service. The choir was truly a worship-leading choir. It was one of the best choirs I have ever encountered, yet it did not come across at all as a performance group. You could tell by their singing and their countenance that they were there to worship and to lead others into worship. There was such a connection between the congregation and the choir. The congregation seemed to experience worship vicariously through the choir's singing. Indeed, on many occasions, when the anthem was familiar, the congregation would rise, and many would begin singing with the choir on the choruses of the songs. There was nothing "showy" about people's worship expressions, but they had freedom and openness to respond to God as He prompted.

The conference was filled with times of worship and teaching. The teaching was on such topics as "The Leader's Passion for God," "The Priority of Worship, "and "Intimacy with God in Worship." Again, it was nothing about form or expression, but a matter of the heart.

God confirmed in my heart during those days in Texas what He wants of me as a worship leader, and now also as a teacher, trainer, resource developer, and encourager of worship leaders. He clearly placed a vision for what worship is to look like in the church I serve. Honestly, I also had struggled with a decision to leave the ministry altogether due to burnout and discouragement. God renewed my call to ministry–I knew I was doing exactly what God wanted me to do.

I had prayed for God to reveal which of the five churches I was to select during this time away, but instead, He chose to give me a clear vision of what the church is to look like and a clear understanding of the importance of working with a pastor who shares this vision for worship. Without such a pastor, I would continue to be very frustrated, knowing God's desire for my leadership, but being hindered by a pastor not being "on the same page." My church was currently in an interim stage, seeking a pastor.

My analytical side began working. I took this "worship template" that God had given me and began placing it on the remaining four churches. The South Carolina church seemed to be, by far, the closest match. But did God want me to go to the closest match, or was God using all of this to show me where He wanted me to be instrumental in leading a congregation of worshippers?

So, what church was God calling me to? After continued prayer, God showed me that His will was for me to stay at the church I had been serving for 13 years and continue to move this church forward in worship renewal. God was calling me to the church I had been serving—a renewed call! I had a real sense that I was exactly where God wanted me, and I loved my job! It had been a long time since I felt so fulfilled in my calling.

The next hurdle was to renew the choir. I saw that as a real key to fulfilling the vision God gave me. We had an amazing, large choir that could handle almost anything I put before them. However, they were more of a performance-oriented choir that needed repurposing (deconstruction) to fit the vision God gave me. God called a new pastor to our church, Gerald Bontrager, who was exactly what our church and I needed in the next chapter of worship renewal. Gerald and I met with the choir, instrumentalists, and others to share with them my journey, sparing very few details. God really used that time to bring renewal to the choir. From that point on, the choir and I had a new beginning, and God did great things with that group. Commitment grew to unheard-of highs for the summer, and excitement was tremendous. I was able to stretch the group, and they were learning and memorizing music at phenomenal speeds. They were taking on the character of a worship-leading choir.

Through this experience I have just shared with you, God renewed my calling to ministry leadership; He renewed my calling to place; and He gave me a new vision for my ministry and began the process of changing me to prepare me for the next calling He would make on my life in about ten more years. **Seeking God for His calling on your life is about building**

your relationship with Him and being willing to be shaped and to sacrifice when needed, and being ready for the most joyful ride of your life at the center of His will!

So often, I wish God would just give me an outline of His plan for my life for the next 20 years. But here's the problem: When we get the road map, we plug it into our life GPS and just go along the path. God wants us to be consistently and daily coming to Him for the next turn in our lives and ministries. The relationship is of utmost importance. However, we find ourselves coming to these times in our lives when we want an easy answer about our calling, to see the handwriting on the wall. God can do that, but in most cases, He wants us to rest in Him and depend on Him for everything we do.

DEFINING WORSHIP LEADING

Once we recognize our calling and God's hand on our lives, we must then equip ourselves to serve Him. Let us consider what a worship leader is and what our role is in the church.

I love Bob Kauflin's definition of a worship leader:

> *A faithful worship leader magnifies the greatness of God in Jesus Christ through the power of the Holy Spirit by skillfully combining God's Word with music, thereby motivating the gathered church to proclaim the gospel, to cherish God's presence, and to live for God's glory.*[51]

Take a moment to dissect this definition and think through ways that you can do this in worship.

This definition makes it clear that a worship leader needs to be intimately familiar with God's Word and combine it with music in the way described. We will look more at some disciplines of worship leaders in a moment.

Brenton Collyer describes the role of a worship leader:

> *The role of a worship leader is to bring the wonder of God into large, vivid focus before the eyes and hearts of our church.*[52]

When people attend worship services we lead, they should encounter the wonder and majesty of God. It should be ever before them.

In our leading worship, we want to help the people come before God to offer pleasing sacrifices of worship and praise to Him. As I mentioned earlier, we are prompters guiding the time of worship. We need to do all we can to remove distractions so that people can respond to God in worship. Remember that the worship team is not to do worship for the people (performers), but rather we are to help them in their worship by serving as prompters, encouragers, and enablers.

I love the way John Piper talks about striving for undistracting excellence:

> *We will try to sing and play and pray and preach in such a way that people's attention will not be diverted from the substance by shoddy ministry nor by excessive finesse, elegance, or refinement. Natural, undistracting excellence will let the truth and beauty of God shine through. We will invest in equipment good enough to be undistracting in transmitting heartfelt truth.*[53]

I must point out here that we need to recognize that **every**

member of our team is intricately important in our worship leadership. The computer tech or audio tech is as much a worship leader as the singer or bass player. Think about which is more of a barrier to your congregation's worship—the bass player missing a few notes or the computer tech displaying the wrong lyrics? I would suggest the wrong lyrics will deter your congregation much more than some missed notes. All members of your team need to understand that their roles are crucial to leading the congregation in worship. All should be well-prepared and execute their roles with a servant's heart.

Before we move on to look at some disciplines worship leaders need to make a part of their lives, let us remind ourselves of the **high calling of worship leadership and the character requirements** the Bible points out for spiritual leaders:

> *Therefore an overseer must be above reproach, the husband of one wife, sober-minded, self-controlled, respectable, hospitable, able to teach, not a drunkard, not violent but gentle, not quarrelsome, not a lover of money. He must manage his own household well, with all dignity keeping his children submissive, for if someone does not know how to manage his own household, how will he care for God's church? He must not be a recent convert, or he may become puffed up with conceit and fall into the condemnation of the devil. Moreover, he must be well thought of by outsiders, so that he may not fall into disgrace, into a snare of the devil. I Timothy 3:2-7*

Is my character in line with my calling as a worship leader?

SOME DISCIPLINES OF WORSHIP LEADERS

These are some important areas of growth for worship leaders. This list is by no means exhaustive, and additional disciplines will be discussed later in the book. While some of these are for the person leading the worship team, many of these naturally translate to ways to help your team improve as worship leaders as well. Some of these points were adapted from an excellent article by David Santistevan.[54]

1. Make worship a daily part of your life.

As mentioned in the first chapter, times of personal worship in a place of solitude is imperative to our growth in Christ and our living out our calling as worship leaders. Who are we when there is no stage, no band, no singers, and no lights? We must spend time reading His Word, praying, and worshipping Him. Spend time singing to God in private. Engage in a reading plan or devotional to help structure your study. Commit Bible passages to memory. If worship is not part of your life, it will be evident on stage.

> **Am I spending time daily worshipping God? Do I need to find someone who can hold me accountable in my walk?**

2. Improve your craft.

Practice your instrument and/or voice. Practice your weak

areas in worship leading, such as speaking, transitioning, and providing flow. Take lessons or otherwise improve your singing or instrumental abilities. Find a good teacher or online courses. Emulate recordings to stretch your skills. A great way to improve is to listen to recordings of yourself and evaluate areas that need improvement. Are you talking too much? Do transitions make sense? Are you playing well and appropriately? Is your singing voice pleasant and appropriate to the style?

What steps do I need to take to improve my craft?

3. **Learn a variety of styles of songs.**

Listen to and learn songs that are not in your style or personal preference. Get familiar with old songs and new songs. Frequently listen to and sing songs that another generation is listening to. All of this will help you in leading intergenerational, multi-ethnic worship as you begin to love and understand other styles of music.

**What style of music do I need
to get more familiar with?**

I had the great opportunity to spend a summer in Kuala Lumpur, Malaysia several years ago assisting and training worship teams in that city. I knew there would be some work with student teams, so I sought and discovered the bands with the greatest influence on student worship in that country. I listened to that music for weeks before going to serve there. It certainly helped me begin to appreciate and worship through other types of music.

4. Model worship and musical excellence in worship.

Worship leaders need to exhibit a lifestyle of worship. As we model this, it will encourage our teams and our congregation to worship with all of their lives. Consider taking time to text your teams with Bible verses you are studying or insights God has given you related to your personal worship. In doing so, you encourage and disciple your team. If you model musical excellence with humility, it will inspire your musicians to a higher level. Conversely, if you are not well-prepared, it will "inspire" your musicians to be poorly prepared.

> **Am I modeling a lifestyle of worship with my team and congregation? Am I modeling musical excellence?**

5. Pastor and disciple your team.

Take time to worship with your team. Disciple them in structured and unstructured ways (more on this later). Share your daily spiritual journey with your team.

6. Embrace the vision of your lead pastor.

Your senior pastor, as mentioned before, is the lead worshipper of the church. Spend time with your pastor, and work together in embracing the vision for the church that God has birthed in him. Having a great relationship with your pastor is important to leading worship effectively at your church.

> Do my pastor and I have a great relationship? Do we understand each other's dreams and passions for the ministries we lead? What do I need to do to improve these areas?

7. Do life with your congregation.

People are not concerned with your slick productions and awesome arrangements. They want to connect with a heart that loves and pursues God. Spend time with your congregation outside of times of gathered worship. Get to know them and help them get to know you. They are much more open to your leadership when there is a relationship with them.

> Are you experiencing life with your congregation outside of your responsibilities as a worship leader?

8. Learn to communicate in front of your congregation.

Some of the most effective worship leaders speak very little. One of the most effective ways to speak is to quote the Bible. Keep your clothing relevant to the congregation you are leading—you don't need to make a fashion statement. I will dive deeply into our spoken communication and our non-verbal communication later in the book.

> **Am I an effective communicator in worship? Does what I wear align with the congregation's attire? Do I call attention to myself?**

9. Pursue an ever-expanding view of God.

David Santistevan noted: "Nothing inspires worship more than amazement. Seek each day to become more and more amazed by the glory of God."[55] A.W. Tozer wrote, "What comes into our minds when we think about God is the most important thing about us."[56]

> **What are you doing to expand your view of God? What books are you reading? What Bible passages are you studying?**
>
> **Which of these nine areas do you need to improve the most? What can you do to work on that area?**

CREATING AN ENVIRONMENT OF UNCONDITIONAL LOVE FOR YOUR WORSHIP TEAM

One aspect of leadership is not mentioned often and is quite important: We must truly love our worship teams.

Several years ago, my approach to missions in an East Asian country markedly changed. While I have done large-scale training in countries around the world (similar to what I do in the United States) my work in that East Asian country had been primarily mentoring and discipling a small group of nationals who had excellent leadership potential and who could make a significant impact on the worship life of their country. In the past years, I have been amazed at how God has used these individuals to train, equip, evangelize, and plant churches in their regions and distant places.

In addition to training, equipping, and resourcing my team of nationals, I feel that one of my greatest, God-given responsibilities is to love and encourage these young men and women. Indeed, that has been a part of my relationship with them in the past years–reminding them that God is sufficient for all they need, nudging them to push beyond their self-imposed limitations, encouraging them (cheering them on) in their good works, and truly loving them like my own children. It is hard to describe the love God has placed in my heart for these people from a different culture, who speak a foreign language, but it is incredibly deep. Our interaction does not stop when I leave their country but continues through weekly communication to offer prayers for their work, encouragement, advice about their struggles, and so much more.

One incident in that ministry revealed to me something

I have never put in my teaching notes nor really taught in numerous seminars, conferences, and events. My national team and I had just finished a three-day event with many worship teams in attendance. In the last hour, people were sharing their significant takeaways from the conference. I had taught a tremendous amount of material, and the response throughout had been awesome. I could tell the people were absorbing and discussing how to put into practice many of the concepts. As I listened to their significant takeaways, I imagined which of the many topics I taught would be beautifully expounded–the spiritual qualities needed in worship team members, how to have great band rehearsals, how to craft beautiful transitions between songs, ways to play better as a band in the sonic spectrum, and I could go on and on.

The answer that astonished me was this one expressed by a worship leader: "I was most impacted by the way the teacher deeply loves his team. I realize I do not show that same love and compassion for my team members. It's not something I ever thought about before as something that I needed, but I see how important it is."

I sat in stunned silence. I never entered that training venue with the thought of demonstrating love for my team members to be an example to others. I never once spoke or taught about the need to show unconditional love for my team. I never even thought about the benefits of loving my team for them to be better worship leaders. I spent weeks preparing the material for those days and countless hours preparing handouts and slides in a foreign language to make the presentation as impacting as possible. This preparation was indeed essential to my work there. But **now I hear that the one thing I didn't prepare for,** the one thing that didn't require musical or worship expertise–unconditional love for my team–may have had the most impact on some who attended.

Oh, the power of our Christian love shown to others! Do you love your worship team deeply? Are you an encourager to them? Are they comfortable sharing life with you? Musicianship is important in worship leading. **But love may be the most important thing we can do to develop our teams into the men and women God wants them to be.** Thanks be to God for the love He has shown us. May God help us exemplify that love in our lives.

> **Do you really love your team members? Do they see that in the way you interact with them? Do they get encouragement and sacrificial love from you?**

GATHERED WORSHIP AND DISCIPLESHIP

When the church talks about discipleship today, it seems so often the conversation goes to small groups, triads, one-on-one mentoring, or perhaps a discipleship class. The fact is that **the greatest tool for discipleship in the church is worship**.

Think about it. If you look at all the people who attend your church and their involvement in the life of the church, I believe you will see that the vast majority do not attend any of the small groups, triads, mentoring, or classes. The majority focus on coming to worship. That indicates that the worship service may be the only time we can really speak into the lives of these church members to form them to be more like Christ. Indeed, we have seen throughout Christian history that the church has considered the worship service to be the primary means of discipleship. Unfortunately, it seems that many churches have lost sight of this and no longer plan worship with intentionality to disciple our people. Worship should bring spiritual formation to the forefront.

We need to think of ourselves as *theological dieticians*.[57] Every song, every prayer, every reading, is feeding the hearts and minds of the people and shaping them spiritually. If you were to ask every person in your church to quote every Bible verse they know from memory and every song they know from memory, most people will know far more songs. That shows us how vitally important it is that the songs we place in their hearts are theologically sound and have no measure of error in them.

Ask yourself this question: **"If all that the people of God had were the worship services we plan and lead, what would they know about Him, and how would they relate to Him?"**[58] We need to make sure every aspect of the worship service is appropriately shaping our people to be more like Christ. That means, not only is our song selection vitally important, but also the content of our prayers and other components of the worship service. Are our public prayers substantive and do they model ways to help our people learn to pray in their times of private worship? Does each component of the service have a positive shaping effect on the congregants?

Everything we do in gathered worship shapes our people's lives and their personal worship throughout the week. As worship leaders, we need to obsess over ways we can better disciple our congregations through times of gathered worship.

> Does being a *theological dietician*, knowing that the corporate worship service may be the only way that the church can disciple its people, make you more keenly aware of your responsibility to plan with great intentionality? What areas do you need to work on first?

BUILDING A DISCIPLE-MAKING WORSHIP MINISTRY

While we do need to see the time of congregational worship as a time of building disciples, we must also consider the many and varied opportunities for making disciples in the worship ministry in the church.

MENTORING

Taking time to mentor others (especially some that may be feeling called to the worship ministry) is so valuable in discipling them, encouraging them, and helping them discern God's call on their lives. God may bring others to mind that you should spend regular time with, to help them in their spiritual journey. I will say more about mentoring in the next section.

SMALL GROUP DISCIPLESHIP

Look for opportunities to form a small group of 3-4 people

to have authentic discipling relationships, where they hold each other accountable. This group does not have to be composed of people in the worship ministry, but could be. You need this for yourself, as well as the others in the group. Replication is a goal in this—that each participant will later form a group of 3-4 people to continue the discipleship journey.

TEAM DISCIPLESHIP

Consider the various groups you lead—some may be small, while others may have vast numbers. Find ways to disciple these groups. One way is through scheduled devotional times, when a rehearsal is stopped, and the group spends some time in worship and Bible study together. Other times that are also important are interruptions in the rehearsal where you may stop a song being sung to talk about a spiritual truth or give testimony related to the lyrics of the song you interrupted. This can help people more passionately connect with the songs they are leading.

ENCOURAGING PERSONAL WORSHIP AND DEVOTION

As mentioned earlier, you can also use technology, such as group texting, blogs, or social media, to share spiritual truths with your team throughout the week. Encourage them and help them think about the things of God during the week to turn their affections to God and improve their times of personal worship. Also, encouraging your teams to worship with the music they will be leading on Sunday will further help their personal worship lives. Additionally, it will help them lead out of an overflow of these personal worship experiences with this music as they lead gathered worship.

Taking time for regular and spontaneous discipleship in the

groups you lead is vitally important.

> **Are you regularly involved in the four varieties of discipleship outlined above? Which areas need work? Make some tangible plans now to make discipleship a priority in your life.**

MENTORING WORSHIP LEADERS

One of the exciting trends I am seeing in worship leadership today is an emphasis on mentoring other worship leaders. Decades ago, a church would call a worship leader to lead all the services of worship at the church and administrate the total worship and music ministry of the church. The expectation was that every song was led by this person. Today, people are seeing the great value of multiplying themselves by mentoring others to be worship leaders. The worship pastor often will take on a coaching and cheerleader role as the worship leaders being mentored have opportunities to lead worship in the services. The worship pastor may be on the platform in a support role, helping with technology, or just joining the congregation in worship. The goal is to make sure the gathered worship is transformative for the church, but how that is publicly led can take on many different forms.

A pastor I once served with said that you can tell you are a good leader if you can walk away and people don't even realize you are absent. This became very real to me the year before I was to leave the country for three months on a missions sabbatical. I spent much time training the worship leadership team in planning and implementing services. I poured into people who could take up the banner of worship leadership so that the church did not miss a beat when I walked away for an extended time.

Today, we are experiencing a great shortage of worship leaders. Part of this may be due to the eradication of graded choir programs in the churches and music programs in the schools. As leaders in our churches, we need to identify people with giftings and callings in worship ministry and do all we can to train, equip, encourage, and provide opportunities for them to lead. We not only are improving worship in the church we serve, but we are preparing worship leaders to send to church plants and international missions opportunities, to help struggling churches, to lead established church worship ministries, and so much more.

We, as worship leaders need to make mentoring worship leaders a high priority in our ministries. Multiplying ourselves should be part of our DNA.

> **Are you currently mentoring one or more people who can lead your team as they lead the congregation in worship? If not, pray that God will reveal someone to you to begin the journey.**

DEVELOPING A MISSIONAL DNA IN YOUR WORSHIP MINISTRY

I believe we would all agree that our churches should not be primarily inward-focused—just taking care of the needs of the church body. Churches that fail to follow the Great Commission and only look inward are churches that die, churches that lose their direction.

As worship leaders, we must seek ways to challenge our teams to always be on mission—getting out of the walls of the church to use their gifts to reach the world for Christ. Here are several ways to consider missional involvement with individuals and teams from the worship ministry:

COMMUNITY SERVICE

Find ways to meet the needs of people in your neighborhood while building relationships that can lead to sharing Christ with others. Find opportunities for your team to work together in sharing God's love in homeless shelters, soup kitchens, local schools, prisons, rehabilitation centers, and similar places. Make time to share these missional experiences in your weekly group times, celebrating the victories and life-change that God provides.

Take your choir, band, or other group to the marketplace to present music and share with people who come by. Go to retirement homes and have a hymn-sing or present some music to help many who feel marginalized and unloved to feel the love of God. Consider other options such as backyard music schools, block parties, or theater-in-the-park.

CHURCH PLANTING/FOSTERING/LOANING MUSICIANS

In my work, I constantly hear of struggling churches desperate to find musicians to help with worship. Consider loaning out some of your musicians to these churches on a rotational basis to bless these churches and help them get healthier.

Some church worship teams are helping with church fostering, where a healthy church comes alongside a struggling church to assist them in many areas. You may be able to develop a worship team to serve that church for a period of time. This is a great way to further develop worship leaders you are mentoring to exercise their skills.

Church planting is so important. Consider raising up a team to go and lead worship at a church plant to help the new work thrive. Whether it is your church or a sister church planting the church, you can be a tremendous help to this new work.

It is hard to release your talented worship team members to serve other places, but it is all part of having a kingdom mindset.

MISSIONS TRIPS AND LONGER SERVICE

A simple way to describe the goal of missions trips is to spread the gospel of Jesus Christ or help other people spread the gospel. As a worship leader, you can involve your team in national and international missions opportunities. Seek out short-term opportunities that partner with missionaries your church supports. Talk with associations and denominations your church may be a part of to find possibilities through those organizations. Seek out ways your worship teams can partner with them in their work through outreach events, training, etc. There are also missions groups like GlobalMissionsProject. com or WorshipConvergence.com that put together short-term missions trips for you or organize trips working with musicians from several churches. They can handle all the logistics for you.

Encourage members of your team to consider serving in a missions position for three months to two years. Mission organizations that you support may have some opportunities for them to serve. Also, encourage your people to consider long-term service in missions.

In the years I served the local church, we were frequently involved in community missions through block parties, outdoor concerts, partnering with other churches to reach struggling neighborhoods, going to nursing homes to sing and share, and more. We took several trips to help our missionaries in another state in many ways, some musical and some not. I took worship teams every couple of years to Asia to lead worship conferences, outreach events, worship services, and other things that missionaries and church leaders in the countries requested. My church granted me a missions sabbatical to serve in a foreign country one summer to help worship teams around the city.

All these things built a missional DNA into our worship ministry. We saw our calling as more than leading worship each Sunday for the local church, but a global calling. I believe our involvement outside the church walls significantly impacted our ability to lead worship from week to week. It also made our personal relationships much closer.

What specific ways can you get your teams on mission in your community, national missions, and international missions? Are there church fostering or planting opportunities in which your church can get involved? Would you consider exploring a missions sabbatical for yourself to go and serve for a short-term assignment?

DEVELOPING A HIGHER LEVEL OF EXCELLENCE IN YOUR WORSHIP TEAMS

In the first part of this chapter, *Understanding Worship Leadership*, we sought to understand what a worship leader is and some disciplines worship leaders should practice. We also discovered that worship leaders need to be theological dieticians to carefully plan and lead worship services that will form participants into the image and likeness of Christ. Another huge part of being a worship leader is to effectively mentor and disciple your team as discussed in the previous material. We should also call out teams to excellence in their service, not only because the Bible demands it, but also because it greatly helps our ability to effectively lead worship that is transformative.

As we consider this, I first take us to an excerpt from Rory Noland's book, *The Heart of the Artist*, where he contrasts the different behaviors and reactions of people serving in the worship ministry who see themselves as merely fulfilling the role of *volunteers* or those who see themselves truly *called* by God to serve their congregation in this way. Read through each dichotomy and see how the different perspectives can make a tremendous difference in your team's ability to lead worship effectively. You also see a deeper level of commitment, joy, and purpose in those that see themselves as called by God to serve.

VOLUNTEER OR CALLED?

1. Volunteers see their involvement at the church as community service, but people called of God see it as a ministry.
2. Volunteers whine about what it is going to cost them, but

people called of God are committed to serving God, period.

3. Volunteers shrink back from resolving relational conflict, but people called of God seek to resolve relational conflict for the sake of unity in the church.

4. Volunteers look at rehearsal as another commitment they are obligated to fulfill, but people called of God look forward to another opportunity to be used by God.

5. Volunteers do little outside practicing or preparation, but people called of God come to rehearsals and worship as prepared as possible, on time and ready to serve Him.

6. Volunteers are not open to constructive criticism; they get defensive about it, but people called of God are grateful for the feedback because they want to be the best they can be for God.

7. Volunteers feel threatened by the talents of others, but people called of God praise Him for distributing gifts and talents as He chooses.

8. Volunteers want to quit at the first sign of adversity or discouragement, but people called of God dig in and persevere.

9. Volunteers find their main source of fulfillment in their talents and abilities, but people called of God know that being used of God is the most fulfilling thing you can do with your life.

10. Volunteers cannot handle being put into situations in which they are going to be stretched, but people called of God respond to God's call with humble dependence on Him.

> After reading through these ten statements,
> would you say you feel *called* or a *volunteer*?
> Which do you act like? What behaviors
> do you see in your team members?

I would encourage you to take some time to have your worship team go through this list and help them discover whether they feel like a *volunteer* or if they feel *called* to the work. You will find some will sense they are called, but yet they truly exhibit the behaviors of a volunteer. Having open discussions about this can help disciple your team in this area.

CREATING A CULTURE FOR BETTER REHEARSALS

This next resource is a great tool in leading your team to be the best they can be. Jon Nichol, of WorshipTeamCoach.com, developed an excellent study that sets a biblical foundation for worship leading with excellence and builds upon that with practical ways those foundations are lived out in worship ministry. With Jon's permission, I have adapted his work for this book.

WHY WE PREPARE

Our primary purpose is to worship God and help others worship God. We do this in four ways:

1. **We minister to the Lord through worship** (Deuteronomy 10:8).
2. **We carry the presence of God** (1 Peter 2:9; Deuteronomy

10:8-9; Colossians 1:27).

3. **We create a place for people to meet with God:**
    - We enhance our environment visually and musically.
    - We eliminate distractions.
4. **We model worship and teach others to worship.**

This requires preparation.

PHILOSOPHY OF PREPARATION

- **Preparation is required for the biblical mandate of skilled musicianship in worship.** Psalm 33:3: *"play **skillfully**"* ... 1 Chronicles 15:22: *"the head Levite in charge of singing ... was **skillful** at it"* ... 1 Chronicles 25:6 - 8: *"all of them trained and skilled in music for the Lord."*
- **Preparation itself is an act of worship.** It is time, talent, and energy given to preparing to serve God and His people. Romans 12:1: *"living and holy sacrifice ... this is truly the way to worship him."* Colossians 3:23-24: *"Work willingly ... as though you were working for the Lord rather than for people."*
- **Preparation allows freedom in worship.** We can be expressive and spontaneous in worship if we are prepared, both individually and as a team.
- **Preparation helps us to provide excellence and beauty.** Philippians 4:8: *"whatever is ... lovely, whatever is admirable if anything is excellent ... think about such things."*
- **Preparation requires both personal and relational investments:** Practice is personal; rehearsal is relational.
  - **Practice is personal.** Each musician and tech needs to learn his/her part before rehearsal. It is an investment both for the worship service and the rehearsal.

- ° **Rehearsal is relational.** Rehearsal is about the team. It is our time together to shape the songs, rehearse the flow of the service, and grow together as a team. If I come unprepared (or don't attend at all), I affect the whole team as well as the worship service.

> Why is great preparation important to worship leadership? Is the idea of coming with all music prepared before arriving at rehearsal foreign to you? To your team?

PRACTICAL REASONS WHY PRACTICE MATTERS
Confidence and freedom in worship

- Preparation = confidence
- Confidence = more freedom in worship
- More freedom in worship = better leadership of and engagement with the congregation

All of that equals a better experience for everyone. Think about this. The more prepared we are to know our music, transitions, etc., the more confidence we have in leading worship. Increased confidence allows us to have more freedom since we are less tied to the musical score. Having more freedom allows us to interact with and truly engage the congregation at a higher level since we are not having to concentrate on notes, rhythms, arrangements, etc. because we know the music so well.

> **Think about times your team has been ill-prepared for leading worship and times they have been well-prepared. How has that felt different in the lives of the worship team? How do you think the congregation experienced the difference?**

PRACTICAL REASONS WHY PRACTICE MATTERS

How well are you and your team preparing your music in personal practice before coming to rehearsal? Rate yourself on this scale:

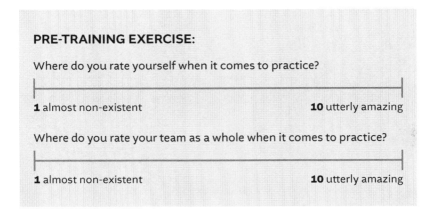

PRE-TRAINING EXERCISE:

Where do you rate yourself when it comes to practice?

1 almost non-existent   **10** utterly amazing

Where do you rate your team as a whole when it comes to practice?

1 almost non-existent   **10** utterly amazing

Here are ways to lead your team to better practice habits:

Model it. Of primary importance in leading your team members to come well-prepared to rehearsals is for you to model what it means to be prepared. You should be the most prepared person in the room. Come knowing your music thoroughly and knowing exactly what you want to do in rehearsal. Get other key team members to also model excellent preparation. If there are times you have not prepared well, do not make excuses—own up to your lack of preparation. Honesty goes a long way.

> **Do you consistently come to rehearsal well-prepared?**

Praise it. When others come well-prepared to rehearsals, praise them and let them know how much you appreciate it. Help people to see how their great preparation makes rehearsal times go so much smoother. Your encouragement goes a long way to reinforce great preparation.

> **Which team members always prepare well? Who is holding the team back due to poor preparation?**

Picture it. Help your team picture what great preparation looks like and why it matters. Later, after your team leads well due to great preparation, point out how much better the experience was for the team and the congregation.

You can help your team picture it by keeping this goal in front of them constantly by using some short statements like:

- Practice is personal; rehearsal is relational.
- We can't lead well what we don't know well.
- If you're called to the worship team, you're called to be skilled. (And skill requires preparation.)

- We are priests creating a space for God and man to meet.

> **What are some ways I can begin to help my team picture what great preparation looks like and what the results might be? What are some recent wins that we can look at to encourage great preparation? What are some short statements that can help create a culture of being well-prepared for rehearsals?**

Clarify it. Be specific about what it looks like to be prepared for rehearsal. Give examples. Avoid setting time limits; some people can reach a high level of preparedness in much less time than others. Setting time limits does not take this into account. Help your people learn how to practice, making best use of their time. Preparing a policy that lays out expectations can be very helpful in communicating these desires with the team. Include expectations for personal practice, rehearsal, sound check/warm-up, and development. (More details on this will come later.)

> **Does your team have any idea of what is expected of them in preparation for rehearsal? How is that communicated? Consider working with team members for buy-in as you develop a preparation policy.**

Expect it. Once the expectations have been clearly communicated, then expect your team members to follow them. Assume the best of your team. Have crucial conversations and lead with love as you confront people who are not preparing and holding the team back. Encourage those who are preparing well. Realize this is a process for some and not something that may happen immediately for everyone. Celebrate the little steps along the way.

> **If your team does know what is expected of them, are you holding them accountable? Do you need to have some hard, but loving conversations with those that are not preparing well?**

EXPECTATIONS FOR PREPARATION

Here are the terms we use as we talk about preparation:

Practice is the personal preparation you put into learning your part and your role in the worship gathering.

Rehearsal is a relational time of joining the pieces of the songs together and connecting the songs into a worship flow.

Soundcheck is the time we take to make sure all the parts of the sound system are working, as well as getting the monitors and the house mixed.

Run-through is more than just a warm-up. It's our time to musically and emotionally prepare to lead worship through music. Our posture and attitude during the run-throughs should be the same as it will be during the worship service.

Start time really means *ready to play* time. Arrive early enough to be ready to play by the posted start time.

Personal development is the ongoing, personal commitment to get better as a musician or tech. It happens through practice, lessons, training events, and other ways you invest in deepening your skill.

PERSONAL PRACTICE EXPECTATIONS

Ask your team to begin learning their songs early in the week to allow enough time to be prepared by rehearsal. They should take time to review the songs within 24 hours of rehearsal and again within 24 hours of services. This will help them come into rehearsal and services with the songs still fresh.

What prepared looks like (use this chart to get a better feel for levels of preparation):

1	2	3	4	5
Conscious Incompetence		Conscious Competence		Unconscious Competence
Learning		Knowing		Mastery

Preparing for rehearsal: Prepare songs to at least a level three by rehearsal. If you're still learning the basics of the song during rehearsal, you aren't contributing your part to the whole. Preparation for rehearsal should include understanding the song form, reading through the rehearsal notes, and listening to the song multiple times (where applicable).

Preparing for services: Prepare songs to a level four or five by the day of corporate worship. The more freedom you have to play and sing your songs without thinking about the mechanics, the more freedom you will have to worship and lead others in worship.

> **Think through the three categories of preparedness and how that affects your ability to lead worship. Do these preparation suggestions seem to make reasonable demands?**

REHEARSAL EXPECTATIONS

1. **Rehearsals are mandatory.** Because of the tremendous importance of attending rehearsals in order to be prepared to lead well in worship, many churches will choose to say that a player who cannot attend the rehearsal will not lead in worship that week. However, there may be cases where the player is greatly needed on the team that week and other provisions must be made, such as meeting with the worship leader at another time to go over everything and get the player ready to play. It is of utmost importance that team members see the rehearsal as a necessary part of preparation.

2. **Be ready to go at the start time.** Team members need to be ready to rehearse at the posted start time of rehearsals. This requires coming in before start time to set up gear, get music, etc.

3. **Notify the worship leader of any overlapping time commitments.** Team members should discuss with the worship leader prior to rehearsal if there is a need to arrive

late to rehearsal or leave early for any reason.

These expectations may seem rather legalistic, but as your team understands the reasons for these, it becomes clear why these standards are needed to help us be the most prepared and therefore have the most freedom to lead worship with excellence.

COMMITMENT TO PREPARATION

Here is one example of a preparation policy. You will need to work with your team to create one for your church.

As a part of the worship team, you are committing to the following:

ON YOUR SCHEDULED WEEK

- Commit to listening and learning the songs at least 24 hours prior to the rehearsal.
- Attend and participate fully in the rehearsal, sound-check, and run-through.
- Arrive early enough to be ready to play at the posted start time.
- Print your music ahead of time, load it on your tablet, or come early to get music from the folder (if applicable).
- Mark your charts for changes, dynamics, problem areas, etc.
- After rehearsal, commit to practicing all the songs within 24 hours of the worship service.
- Arrive with enough time to complete any set-up before the worship sound check and the run-through.

MONTHLY

- Commit time each month to personal development (set

goals). Here are some suggestions:

- ° Read an article on your instrument.
- ° Watch a training video.
- ° Meet with a more experienced player/singer for mentoring.
- ° Invest in short-term private lessons or coaching sessions to learn a specific skill.

YEARLY

- Commit to attending at least one skill development workshop or seminar.

ACCOUNTABILITY

Commitment to serve in this worship ministry means a commitment to these expectations for preparation. These expectations are for team members and leaders alike. As a team, we need to hold each other accountable to these standards. But we do so with grace and assuming the best in others, while not shying away from crucial conversations where we need to speak the truth.

A document such as this gives us a common standard to work toward and to encourage each other to work toward.

> Begin now to make a plan on who will help you create a document of this type for the worship ministry at your church. What will be included? How will it be communicated? How will people be held accountable?

Remember, as you begin to implement these things, always keep the reason for the standards before your team. Without great preparation, it is difficult for us to have the freedom we need to help the congregation along in the journey of worship. We are to remove distractions that can hinder the time of worship. Unpreparedness is one of the worst distractions. Holding each other accountable to high standards as we live out our calling helps us to be better used by God in leading His people in worship.

Planning Worship

Having laid the foundations of worship and worship leadership, we are now ready to build on those concepts. In this chapter, we will consider how to plan worship services that engage the people of God in transformational worship. The planning process is vital to the worship life of the congregation. As we plan worship, we seek God's plan and utilize the great number of tools at our disposal to flesh out the journey of congregational worship.

THE FORMATS OF WORSHIP

Formats of worship are related to the structure or form of a worship service and the components used in those services. It is important for the worship planner to have some knowledge of these forms to provide additional tools and resources for planning worship for the local church body.

There are four formats of worship:

LITURGICAL

The liturgical service is organized around the church year and usually follows a predictable weekly format or *liturgy* (meaning *the work of the people*). The service is formal in structure. There is generally much congregational participation in singing, reading of prayers, creeds, the Lord's Supper, and more. The service is organized around the Bible texts dictated by the lectionary, a book that lists a collection of Scripture readings appointed for specific Sundays of the church year. It includes an Old Testament reading, a Psalm, a New Testament reading, and a Gospel reading for each week.

Integral to the liturgical service is the *Christian* year, a cycle of seasons and holy days that commemorate the life, death, and resurrection of Jesus. The lectionary is organized around the seasons and holy days of the Christian year; the readings come in three cycles covering three years. In the course of all the lessons, the entire witness of the Bible will be presented to the church. There is an excellent intentionality and discipleship plan in utilizing the church year and the lectionary in worship. It helps people engage in the gospel message of Jesus Christ and exposes them to the breadth of God's Word. Too often, churches fail to spend much time reading the powerful Word of God in their services of worship. They cherry-pick Scriptures to the point that the church only hears a select part of God's Word each year. They focus on secular holidays rather than celebrating the holy days of the Christian year. These problems are greatly reduced in the liturgical tradition. You can find a church year calendar at WorshipMinistryGuidebook.com.

Let me illustrate ways a connection with the Christian Year in worship can be a benefit to your congregation:

I grew up thinking the five significant days of the church year were Christmas, Easter, Mother's Day, Father's Day, and the United States' Independence Day. They were undoubtedly the days that seemed to receive the most excitement and specialness in my traditional Baptist roots. Since my childhood, I have been exposed to and studied many different worship traditions. I have found that we often fall short of the wonderful experiences we can have in worship because we have eliminated much of the traditional church calendar. In our effort to move away from some of the excesses of other traditions of Christianity, we have "thrown out the baby with the bath water" (another expression I learned growing up!).

Let's look at a period of time in the Christian Year—the season of Lent. Ash Wednesday marks the beginning of the season of Lent. The 40-day Lenten period is characterized by prayer and preparation to celebrate Easter. Since Sundays celebrate the resurrection of Jesus, the six Sundays that occur during Lent are not considered part of the 40 days of Lent and are referred to as the *Sundays in Lent*. The number 40 is connected with many biblical events, but especially with the forty days Jesus spent in the wilderness preparing for His ministry by facing the temptations that could lead him to abandon his mission and calling.

Lent ends with Holy Week, beginning the Sunday before Easter and going up to Easter Sunday. The Sunday before Easter is Palm Sunday or Passion Sunday and generally celebrates Jesus' triumphal entry into Jerusalem. The Thursday is Maundy Thursday or Holy Thursday and remembers the last supper. Good Friday is the day that we commemorate Christ's death on the cross. Finally, Easter Sunday is the day we celebrate the resurrection.

Lent has traditionally been marked by penitential prayer, fasting, and almsgiving. Christians today use the Lenten season for introspection, self-examination, and repentance. Some churches still fast on specific days during Lent, especially giving up meat, sweets, and other types of food. I often give up something during Lent. For instance, I have given up soft drinks and sweet tea, only to drink water (I have a hard time without my sweet tea!). I have discovered that every time I crave tea or a soft drink, I think about why I am giving up this beverage and focus on the suffering and death of Jesus. It is incredible how much this helps me get in focus and prepare for Easter. Other traditions do not place as great an emphasis on fasting but focus more on charitable deeds, especially helping those in physical need with food and clothing or simply giving money to charities. Most Christian churches that observe Lent at all focus on it as a time of prayer, especially penance, repenting for failures and sin, as a way to focus on the need for God's grace. It is a preparation to celebrate God's marvelous redemption at Easter and the resurrected life that we live and hope for as Christians.

In my opinion, unless we truly experience Lent, Easter is not nearly as grand a celebration. Still, the idea may seem somewhat foreign to many who have never been exposed to the "real" church calendar. To further illustrate how we can tap into this tradition to benefit our congregations, here are some ways that you can help your congregation in their personal worship and their times of congregational worship in the Lenten season:

- Prepare a 40-day (or 46-day) Lenten devotional or even a Holy Week (8-day) devotional for the entire congregation to share. You can assign various members of the body to write the devotionals to make them more personal for your church.

- Encourage your congregation to go through a daily Bible

reading plan for Lent.

- Plan an Ash Wednesday service.
- Include Lenten devotionals in your weekly bulletin or newsletter.
- Plan all your Sunday worship services during the season to have a Lenten focus. Perhaps choose a song that will tie the time together each week.
- Plan special Holy Week services: Palm Sunday, Maundy Thursday, and Good Friday.
- Display various types of art with a Lenten emphasis around the church. Find excellent art for your bulletin or screens in worship.
- Distribute nails or small crosses to each person to keep with them throughout Lent as a reminder of the season.
- Encourage families to observe Lent at home. There are numerous resources on the web to give you ideas.

There are excellent resources to use to make these special days come alive for worshippers. The preceding thoughts are intended to help the reader see the values in the liturgical format and traditions that accompany it.

THEMATIC

The thematic service is created with the idea that every element should support the theme for the day. The sermon topic usually makes that determination. Then all Scripture readings and songs will relate to that theme. Some churches may take it even further by having short videos, graphics, set designs, and other things which relate to the theme of the day. As a worship planner in a thematic format, you would be given the sermon topic by your pastor; then, you would select songs from your congregation's song list, and perhaps songs not known to them, to utilize in worship. All other elements of worship would be chosen with the theme in mind.

A great benefit of this worship format is that when congregants leave the worship service, they should be well acquainted with the theme for the day. The "big idea" for the day would be effectively communicated.

There are also downfalls to this format in that finding supporting songs for some topics, like "grace," or "heaven," might be simple, but many topics are nearly impossible for which to find songs related to the theme. In addition, narrowing the entire service to a single topic can inadvertently cause missing out on the expanse of worship needed to help people encounter the glory of God, the depravity of sin, and the grace He provides. We may eliminate expressions that the body needs that Sunday due to constricting our choices to a narrow field.

Both liturgical and the thematic services are made up of discrete elements, often with no logical flow. A song may be followed by a prayer, another song, announcements, a children's sermon, another song, an offertory instrumental song, a choir presentational song, a video, a sermon, another song, and another announcement time. This is not uncommon in many churches with a thematic worship format. This is a prevalent format in traditional worship styles as well.

The third format seeks to eradicate disjointed elements of worship and create more flow and a feel of a journey in worship.

FREE-FLOWING PRAISE

In a service with a format of free-flowing praise, the music and sermon may be totally independent (no thematic relationship). In this format, there may be one or more continuous sections of singing. For example, a segment of uninterrupted singing could last 10-50 minutes. Sustained times of singing require more planning, skill, and insight to carry them out effectively, but they can be quite meaningful in worship.

Contemporary styles of worship today follow this format. In many services, the main components of the service are a section of singing followed by a sermon. There may be a brief welcome and announcements, but often little else. Probably the most significant attribute of this format is the emphasis on a seamless flow in the service.

I find great value in all three formats of worship. I believe that blending these three formats has excellent value for the church today. That leads to the fourth format of worship.

CONVERGENCE

A worship planner who follows the convergence format will draw from any or all of these traditions in creating the worship service. For instance, a service might be created around Pentecost Sunday, focusing on the coming of the Holy Spirit on the appropriate Sunday. We might select a single congregational song or presentational song that fits the theme for the sermon. A great creed from the liturgical tradition might be used that is powerful when read together as a congregation during gathered worship. Flow, rather than a disjointed feel in worship, is created by borrowing from the free-flowing praise format. We can find exceptional value and provide fresh experiences in worship by finding great pieces in each format.

> Look at the worship plan at your church. Does it look the same from week to week, with just different songs and sermon titles? In what ways can a move to a convergence style of worship breathe new life into services that might get stale from doing the same thing over and over?

SONGS FOR WORSHIP

I often refer to songs as a vital part of our *worship vocabulary* — they help us express our worship to God. As long as we are singing songs we know, we are able to worship without the hindrance of learning new melodies and rhythms. When we place a new song in our times of corporate worship, we can interrupt the flow of worship. When new songs are first introduced, the people have to take their eyes off the Lord and concentrate on the task of learning the new tune. With this in mind, I believe new songs can kill our worship, but they can also greatly enhance our worship. Let's look at this in more depth.

WHY LEARN NEW SONGS?

Scripture calls us to "sing a new song to the Lord." Here are a few examples:

- Sing to Him a new song; play skillfully and shout for joy. Psalm 33:3 (NIV)
- He put a new song in my mouth. Psalm 40:3 (NIV)
- Oh sing to the Lord a new song. Psalm 96:1
- I will sing a new song to you, O God. Psalm 144:9

- Praise the Lord! Sing to the Lord a new song. Psalm 149:1

Singing new songs is not simply for the sake of novelty. New songs are beneficial because they keep us out of a rut, bring us a new sense of freshness and enthusiasm, force us to think about what we are singing, expand our worship vocabulary and help us capture what God is saying to the body at the time. Newer, contemporary songs generally will connect to today's culture in a language they understand better than songs several decades or centuries old.

New songs are vital to a church's worship. So we turn now to discover the best places to find new songs and how to determine if these potential songs are the best songs for your church.

> **Does your church incorporate new songs into its body of songs used in worship?**

FINDING SONGS

As you begin searching for the best new songs to introduce to your congregation, remember that your church's worship DNA is not the same as the church down the street or the one you watch on YouTube. Knowing your congregation is vitally important to selecting the right songs. The first step in finding great songs for worship is discovering the possibilities. Listed below are sources to search for songs that might work at your church. Next, we will look at filters to determine if the song is right for your congregation.

You will find hyperlinks and updates to this list at Worship-

MinistryGuidebook.com

SOURCES FOR MODERN WORSHIP SONGS

Take time browsing through the most popular/best-sellers to find the most used songs in churches today. This provides a pool of POTENTIAL songs.

- **Discover the CCLI top 100 songs.** Particularly note the additional listing of the top 100 SBC songs. Check out the lists with audio.
- **Look at LifeWayWorship.com.** Note their best sellers.
- Browse and listen to music at **PraiseCharts.com**. Note their top lists as well.
- To make the three areas above easier for you, we compile a weekly list of **the top 20 songs from CCLI, LifeWay Worship and PraiseCharts**. Check out the weekly "Top 20 Worship Songs" — your weekly worship vitamin. A bonus is that audio links are provided for all the CCLI songs.
- **Get recommendations from other worship leaders.** Find leaders at churches similar to your church and see what is resonating with their congregation.
- **Listen to worship song-based Christian radio stations.** Some of the popular songs on the radio are suitable for congregational singing, but some are not. (See *Evaluating Songs* in the next section). If a large percentage of your congregation listens to Christian radio, introducing some of these songs will find quicker learning.
- **Listen to worship music on Spotify, Amazon, iTunes, etc.**
- **Attend worship conferences and other worship events.** Follow up (find the source) immediately on great songs you

hear in these settings that might work in yours.

- **Check out songs from People and Songs.**

CONTEMPORARY ARRANGEMENTS OF OLDER HYMNS

While keeping the same tune and lyrics, contemporary arrangements provide a fresh, usually more band-driven approach to the timeless hymns. Often these breathe new life into old hymns.

- **LifeWayWorship.com** has an immense catalog of contemporary arrangements of traditional hymns. Go to FIND MUSIC and click CONTEMPORARY HYMN in the SHOW ONLY section and listen to the arrangements.
- **HymnCharts.com** has a large catalog of over 150 hymn arrangements in contemporary styling with tremendous resources, including many multitracks that support the arrangements. You can find many of these arrangements with fewer supporting products on PraiseCharts.com.
- **PraiseCharts.com** also has a number of contemporary hymn arrangements to search through. Be sure to check out their PraiseHymns series.

MODERN HYMNS

Today's hymn writers are producing some great songs for our congregations that are theologically rich and very singable. Here are some great sources to check out. Many of these songs can also be found on LifeWayWorship.com and PraiseCharts.com to give you full support products.

- **Getty Music**
- **CityAlight**

- **Sovereign Grace Music**
- **Stuart Townend**

> ### Take some time to get familiar
> ### with these resources for new songs.

Once you have found some potential candidates for new songs to introduce to your church, you must first put them through rigorous evaluation to ensure they are suitable for your congregation.

EVALUATING SONGS

Remember from the section on discipleship in corporate worship that people recall more songs than Bible verses. The songs we use teach theology, so we need to be very discerning in the ones we introduce to our congregation. Evaluating songs is far more than just choosing a song because we like how it sounds or because it is popular. Just because others use the song does not mean it is acceptable for your church. I have adapted an excellent evaluative tool by Scott Christensen to help us in this process.[61] Additionally, The Berean Test is a great tool for analyzing lyrics biblically (TheBereanTest.com).

EVALUATING THE LYRICS OF EACH SONG

OBJECTIVE CRITERIA: LYRICS — WHERE BIBLICAL PRINCIPLES MUST CONTROL THE CONTENT OF THE WORDS (JOHN 17:17)

Are the lyrics biblically and doctrinally sound? Do the lyrics distinctively and accurately reflect biblical language or ideas? Do they contain Scripture and/or scripturally inspired thoughts? Do the lyrics reflect sound theology and Christian practice? Note: There could be one line in the song that can disqualify the song from use.

Are the lyrics spiritual and God-centered? Do the lyrics stimulate spiritual reflection and contemplation of truth? Do they induce genuine praise, thanksgiving, contrition and joy that is God-directed? Does the song leave one delighting in God's character and deeds or upon ourselves and/or worldly values? Worship must glorify God.

Are the lyrics clear and understandable? Do the lyrics clearly communicate the message in an understandable way? Is the message obscured by outdated language or overly popular language that will soon be outdated? Is there an enduring quality to the words chosen?

Additionally, are the words specifically Christian? Some song lyrics are so vague that they could be sung about any religion's god.

In addition, if you are not the senior pastor, I would **ask the senior pastor to sign off on any new song** to make sure he confirms the usability of the song.

EVALUATING THE MUSIC OF EACH SONG

SUBJECTIVE CRITERIA: MUSIC – WHERE PERSONAL PREFERENCES MUST BE GUIDED BY BIBLICAL PRINCIPLES (PHILIPPIANS 4:8):

Is it wholesome? Does the musical style reflect worldly values or those which can be distinctively identified with historic standards of artistic truth, dignity and beauty?

Is it excellent and creative? Does the music meet standards of excellence? Does it have a well-crafted form with a good melody, harmony and rhythm? Is it original and artistic, rather than formulaic or trite? God is glorified by giving Him our best. However, our goal is not perfectionism but God's honor. Furthermore, worship is not mere conformance to some external standard but must come from the heart (Mark 7:6-7).

Is it memorable and singable? Does the song have a memorable tune? Does the music help one to remember the lyrics lodging its truth in the heart and mind?

Does the song lend itself to the average person to learn and sing? Does it have a reasonable melody and rhythm that allows for easy congregational singing, or can it be adapted for such? Is the vocal range within acceptable limits for most people to sing? (I will discuss this in detail a bit later). Congregational singing should not require professional abilities.

Is it compatible? Does the music fit the lyrics? Do the two go well together as an appropriate expression of the message or meaning of the song? Does the music lend itself to the spirit and content of the lyrics for worshipping God that is distinct from music for mere enjoyment? Does the music hinder or enhance the message of the lyrics, given the particular kind of emphasis (e.g., the mood — joyful, solemn, majestic, etc.)?

EVALUATING YOUR BODY OF SONGS (ON YOUR SONG LIST)

In addition to having songs with great lyrics and appropriate music, we need to utilize a variety of songs in worship. Look at the songs on your song list and consider these points:

Are the lyrics of the songs addressed to the heart and mind (i.e. songs that provoke proper affections of the heart as well as godly intellectual reflection)? Is there a balance between songs that are weighty and thought-provoking (i.e. songs that focus on deep truths) as well as those that are simple (but not trivial), meditative, repetitive (e.g. note Psalm 136) and responsive in nature?

Are the lyrics marked by variety? Do the lyrics reflect a balance in emphasis (Ephesians 5:19 and Colossians. 3:16 — psalms, hymns and spiritual songs)? Do they reflect songs addressing God directly (first and second person) as well as those which speak about God (third person)? Do they focus on God's character as well as His deeds? Do they reflect doctrine and theology (what we believe) as well as experience and practice (what we do)? Do they emphasize a corporate dimension (the church) as well as a personal dimension? Do they reflect the wide variety of responses of worship (i.e., contrition, thankfulness, joy, praise, peace, celebration, reflection, exaltation, etc.)? Is the variety of songs primarily devoted to God as the subject (rather than ourselves)? God is the focus of our worship.

Are the songs stylistically balanced? Does the music reflect a balance and variety of different styles (Ephesians 5:19 and Colossians 3:16) and instruments (Psalm 150) that communicate to a broad range of tastes and aesthetics (e.g., older as well as newer) while retaining wholesome and excellent values? Is there a balance between historic hymns and songs as well as contemporary songs and musical styles? Is there an appreciation and utilization of the wide variety of aesthetic expressions and creative abilities God has endowed us with? Personal preference should not be elevated to the status of a biblical principle, thus promoting legalism. Scripture nowhere commands a particular musical style (Mark 7:8-9, 13). Believers should respect and defer to the tastes and preferences of others and not seek merely their own (Philippians 2:3-4).

Song selection
Choose songs that:

- Are God-honoring, Christ-centered, and biblically rich.
- Have texts about God, not just ourselves.
- Allow us to sing to God. (vertical)
- Allow us to exhort one another. (horizontal)
- Are the ones your church family will connect with.

EVALUATING THE MELODY

Congregationally-friendly keys. Leading songs in keys that are too high for the average singer is perhaps one of the most significant "transgressions" of worship leaders, which leads to creating congregational spectators rather than participative worshippers. This is a problem witnessed in a large percentage of churches that use modern worship songs.

I was attending a church that had an incredible band and vocal team. I had been told that the worship music at that church was awesome. Well, it was excellent in its musical perfection, but I noticed almost no one singing in the congregation. One of the primary reasons was that the songs were being sung in keys too high for most people.

Many worship leaders feel it is best to sing the songs in the original keys in order to sound more like the original recording. **As worship leaders, our calling is not to sound like the original recording but it is to help our people voice their worship and praise.** Sometimes that means sacrificing our ideal sound to facilitate a better environment for worship.

CRITICAL UNDERSTANDING
Our responsibility is to enable the congregation to sing their praises, not to showcase our great platform voices by pitching songs in our power ranges.

For people to sing the songs of worship, the songs have to be pitched in keys that the ordinary person can sing. If songs are too high, many people stop singing because it hurts to sing high. Some drop the key an octave for portions of the song if the music is pitched really high. The problem is that the average singer has a medium range, and many worship leaders have high voices and want to pitch the songs in keys in which they sound the best.

Worship is not about impressing the congregation with our extraordinary vocal skills; rather, as worship leaders, our task is to enable others to worship.

So what is a "singable melody?" How is a congregationally-friendly key determined?

The melody should be attainable by the "average" singer. In studies of the human voice and ranges for males and females (soprano, alto, tenor, and bass) as well as observations by many leaders, here's the bottom line—**the sweet range of the average voice is the octave C to C.** Seek to pitch song melodies with an octave range in this zone and the vast majority of your congregation will be able to sing it well.

However, many songs cannot be contained in that octave. **In those cases, select keys for songs with the lowest melody note the congregation will sing at an A. The highest note should be**

a D (or an occasional Eb). The "Eb" should only occur on rare occasions and not be sustained. The average person will struggle with E and above. (This is such an important concept that I have participants in my worship conferences raise their right hands and pledge that they will never again lead the congregation in inappropriate keys!) If parts of the song stay at the high end of that range for a

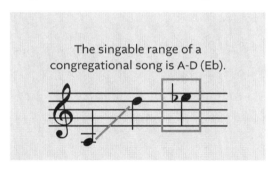

The singable range of a congregational song is A-D (Eb).

lengthy period, it will tire voices fast, so those songs need lower-key considerations if the lowest note in the range is within acceptable limits. Do not assume that a song's "original key" is a good key for maximum participation of congregations.

Also, if a song has a narrow range and can be acceptable in several keys, and if the song is originally sung in a higher key, I would tend to pitch that song in one of the higher acceptable keys for the congregation to retain the energy of the original music.

You will find examples of songs and how to determine the best keys at WorshipMinistryGuidebook.com. Also, there is a link to a table with these keys already selected for you for over 200 most popular songs.

Memorable melody/easy to learn. Does the music help one remember the lyrics, placing its truth in the heart and mind? I have been in a worship service where a new song was introduced, and we sang the song for at least seven minutes. After the song was complete, I could not have sung the melody back to you. It was so unmemorable. The songs we use should be ones that will stick in the minds and hearts of the congregants for days and years to come.

Good marriage with lyrics. Do the music and the lyrics go well together as an appropriate expression of the message or meaning of the song? Does the music lend itself to the spirit and content of the lyrics for worshipping God rather than music for mere enjoyment? Does the melody hinder or enhance the message of the lyrics?

> A worship leader's calling is to help the people sing with all their being, even at the sacrifice of some things we, as musicians, would prefer. A worship leader's calling may require musical sacrifice for the sake of the congregation.

> After working through all these ways of evaluating songs used in worship, what areas do you need to work on?

CAN WE SING SONGS FROM QUESTIONABLE SOURCES?

There is much talk among church leaders related to whether we should sing songs coming out of various churches that are embroiled in controversy or known heresies. At the time of this writing, out of the top 10 songs on the CCLI top 100 list, eight of those songs came from two churches that are often at the forefront of this controversy.

There seem to be two currents of thought on this issue:

1. Many people are excluding these songs because of the problems with the churches from which they were born—whether due to heresy or scandals in leadership.
2. Others believe that the vessel which creates the song (composer, church, ministry) should not determine the merit of the work—the song should be judged in and of itself.

Let's consider these points in determining if we can sing their songs:

> **Realize the songs we sing in worship are vitally important to the building of disciples in our congregations.**

Many people are not part of a discipleship group. Many do not meet with other Christians except for corporate worship. Many never open their Bibles during the week. The corporate worship service for them is our primary means of discipleship. Songs are a significant part of that process. We are discipling our congregations through the music we select, so we must guard our song selection by choosing appropriate songs. Therefore, the messages we place in the hearts of our people need to be closely monitored.

> **The songs we use must be biblical and line up with your church's doctrine and beliefs.**

Does the song relay truth without error? Review the

evaluative tools I shared with you earlier for determining the worth of song lyrics for your church. If there is anything in the song that does not line up with the Word of God, eliminate it.

> **If the source of the song is in question, this does not taint whether or not truth is expressed in the song.**

If you have determined that the song is indeed biblical, then singing it would not harm your church members' theology nor infuse them with heresy.

Many would argue that if you begin to rule out songs written by questionable sources, you would have to eliminate many well-loved songs like *It Is Well with My Soul* because its author eventually denied hell, affirmed purgatory, and taught universalism, or *Come Thou Fount of Every Blessing* whose pastor author left the faith. The author of many of the Psalms, David, was an adulterer and arranged for someone to be murdered. If we are determined to remove any songs from questionable sources, we would perhaps lose a significant portion of our songs if we could accurately assess the holiness, beliefs, and righteous living of all those responsible for the creation of the songs we sing. I am reminded of Jesus' words, "Let Him who is without sin cast the first stone." We see throughout history that God uses imperfect people for His purposes.

As Mike Harland states in his article, *Can We Sings Their Songs?*:

> *If a song says something that is biblically true it is not because the writer received some kind of revelation of truth now captured in a song. It is because the truth of the song was settled by God*

Himself and was true before the song was written and will be true after it is forgotten. Truth is eternal and the songs we sing in worship should bear the markers of His truth. The truth they express should never be attributed to a human author as if the writer came up with it. If a song is true, then God is the One who made it true.[62]

Well, what about the fact that singing their songs provides financial support to these ministries, which we cannot condone?

That is probably the best argument currently being made as a reason to eliminate the songs from questionable sources. As we report our song usage to CCLI and purchase music and tracks of these songs, royalties flow to the copyright owners of the songs, supporting their ministries.

However, if you follow this argument, you would have to stop buying many of the products you currently purchase because of the causes those manufacturers support that oppose the biblical worldview. You would have to divest yourself of funds in your retirement account that invest in companies that don't meet your godly ideals. You would have to quit watching Disney movies or going to one of their theme parks. You would have to boycott many of the stores you frequent due to their support of anti-biblical issues. You would have to give up most social media platforms that you may utilize. As you can see, this line of thinking, if followed, would radically change our lives. That is not to say that it is a wrong way of thinking–just a question as to why we would only practice this with worship songs while ignoring all the other similar issues.

BOTTOM LINE

Each church must carefully weigh the issue and determine if they feel using songs from these sources hurts their churches. I do not believe that God holds us responsible for what a songwriter believes, but He does hold us accountable for the diet of songs we give to our congregations–that we give them songs full of truth without error.

Mike Harland says it well: *Don't die on this hill. There is not a single writing team in the world that, if your leaders asked you not to sing their songs, would result in the collapse of your ministry. Pursue unity and understanding on this question, and take care of your flock at all costs.*[63]

If your church leadership feels you need to eliminate songs from a particular source, realize that there are hundreds of excellent songs your congregation can sing without using those songs. Seek to create unity in whatever is decided.

My friend, David Manner, said, "All congregations absolutely have the responsibility to filter their songs biblically and doctrinally, and church unity should also be considered in those selections. But if one chooses to sing songs by certain authors or composers and another chooses not to, it is a false dichotomy to claim one is or will be theologically suspect and the other righteous."[64]

> **Do your church leaders need to discuss this? How do you feel about singing songs from questionable sources?**

MODERN SONGS FOR INTERGENERATIONAL WORSHIP

As we strive to lead unified worship with multiple generations, I pose this question: **How do we select from the vast field of modern worship songs those songs of excellence which can best engage people with more contemporary song preferences AND those with more traditional song preferences?** Getting this right can make great strides in pulling together all generations in meaningful times of unified worship.

Some of the same qualities that help all congregations to sing well are necessary to engage the older congregants—**key selection and song familiarity**. As outlined earlier, songs must be in attainable keys for seniors to want to sing them. Familiarity is a huge factor that I will address more later in the book. How we introduce songs, how we repeat them with intentionality, and how many songs are on our song list are all critical areas of consideration for engaging the older generation. Paring down our song lists for more repetition of songs is often needed (more on this later).

Songs that are **difficult to sing** due to lots of syncopation, difficult melody shifts, etc., should be avoided. **Singing sections of a song ad nauseam** can turn off older adults (and others as well). Just because the recording repeats the bridge nine times does not mean that that amount of repetition is good for the local church. Every church is different.

Utilizing **contemporary arrangements of old hymns** while maintaining the basic rhythms and melodies of the originals is a great place to bring multiple generations together. Also, so many modern hymns sung by the church today are songs embraced well by all generations.

As a worship planner, always consider the people you lead in worship. You need to have a pastoral heart of uniting the body rather than dividing the body. Don't just cater to one generation exclusively.

Do you serve an intergenerational congregation? If so, are you being sensitive to song selection and execution that helps everyone to worship well?

NEW SONGS: A WORSHIP ENHANCER OR WORSHIP KILLER?

Earlier, I indicated that it is necessary for us to sing new songs in worship—they can significantly enhance our times of worship. However, new songs can also be a detriment to worship.

On one extreme, in many contemporary worship services, worship leaders introduce several new songs in a single service. For this reason, the congregation ceases its participatory worship to 1) learn the new song; or 2) turn totally to spectator mode and treat the song as a "special music" portion of the service. In churches with more than one worship leader/planner, this problem worsens with inadequate coordination of songs used in worship.

On the other extreme, in some traditional worship services, there is a reluctance to use any contemporary worship songs. This ignores the biblical mandate, the blessings of connecting with what God is doing *today* in worship music, and the ability to use expressions that better connect with much of today's culture.

So how do we balance the problem of creating spectators with all the great reasons to include new songs in our worship?

> **The key is how we introduce the songs and the frequency of new song introductions.**

HOW MANY NEW SONGS SHOULD WE SING?

First, **NEVER introduce more than one new song in a worship service**. Otherwise, you greatly risk interrupting the flow and momentum of worship. In looking at numerous churches and experiences, it can be determined that singing more than one new song in a service is a significant detriment to worship. This is the second area I have worship training participants raise their right hands for a pledge and say that they will never have a congregation sing more than one new song in the worship service. Just in case it didn't stick the first time, it is worth repeating:

> **NEVER introduce more than one new song in a worship service.**

Second, **the number of new songs you should introduce in a given month will depend upon your congregation's level of new song "tolerance."** Each congregation is different regarding the number of new songs they can process in a given amount of time, so be sensitive and watch for signs of new song "burn-out" (i.e., a significant drop in the level of participation). For some churches, **one song a month may be enough**; for others, two a month is reasonable.

> **Do you need to adjust the number
> and frequency of new song use?**

INTRODUCING NEW SONGS

How we introduce new songs can make an extreme difference in how well the congregation embraces the song. Here are some ways to introduce new songs:

1. **Begin your service with the new song.**

The new song will not interfere with the forward movement of worship if it comes at the beginning. You can follow the new song with a familiar one and continue your progression of worship. It is also best to repeat the verse and/or chorus several times. This way, the melody and lyrics have a better opportunity to imprint themselves on the congregation's hearts and minds.

2. **If you want to use the song later in the service, introduce it before the worship service begins.**

Tell the congregation that this is a new song, which you will be singing again later in the service, and you want everyone to get familiar with it before the worship begins. Then sing through a verse and a chorus (which you can do with just the acoustic guitar or keyboard). In a sense, you open worship with a teaching time — introducing a new song that can be used later in worship.

3. The new song needs to be sung several weeks in a row.

This concept is often overlooked by worship leaders and is one of VITAL IMPORTANCE. One-third or more of your church is absent on a given Sunday. Other circumstances reduce the overall attendance numbers on any given Sunday. Use the *Rule of 3-1-1* or *2-1-1*. Repeat a new song for two or three consecutive Sundays and then give it one Sunday of rest. Add it back to worship the following Sunday and see how well the congregation has learned it. With this kind of repetition, you are helping the congregation take on the song as part of its worship vocabulary. Unfortunately, if you do the song for one week and then skip a month or more, the song may seem new all over again. It is imperative that you use repetition in learning the new song!

4. Introduce new songs in small group settings before you use them with your congregation.

When more people are familiar with the song, the congregation grasps the new song much more quickly. Teach the song in youth worship venues, small group Bible studies, choirs, men's groups, or any other smaller setting that occurs in your church's life. The more people who know the song before you introduce it in worship, the better the experience will be.

5. Introduce the new song as "presentational music/special music."

A soloist, choir, or ensemble could sing the song the Sunday before using it with the congregation. A nice instrumental arrangement can help people learn the tune.

6. Play a recording of the new song as people gather for worship.

You can select ten new songs to introduce in the coming months and have them played as people gather for worship. Little by little, the people become familiar with the songs before the songs are formally introduced in worship.

7. Create a webpage with a virtual jukebox of upcoming worship songs.

Create a webpage of upcoming worship songs using Spotify or YouTube videos embedded or linked on the church's website. As long as you are using Spotify audio or YouTube videos, you do not need to secure licenses. To legally embed your in-house audio files, you would need a license (for a streaming license to cover this, check out the CCS streaming license). Begin with only about ten songs, so people will first focus on those.

8. Create digital media or downloads of new songs for distribution.

If your church obtains the CCLI Rehearsal License, you can create a means of digital distribution (CDs, flash drives, download links, etc.) for your congregation of the upcoming new songs. Distribute these to your congregation and ask them to spend time with the songs, getting familiar with them and worshipping with them in their personal worship times. Be sure to provide excellent congregationally-friendly arrangements in keys ordinary people can sing in. The best resource to find congregational worship songs that are accessible to the average person is LifeWayWorship.com. They have great audio files of all their arrangements that you could use in church to mirror what your congregation is listening to. For example, you could: 1) Begin with the first ten new songs from a new song introduction timeline to produce the first songs for mass distribution. This project should ideally go out at least four weeks before you begin introducing these new songs. 2) Plan a second distribution for the following ten songs several weeks later. This will accelerate your ability to engage your congregation with new songs in worship.

9. Prepare a weekly guide.

A weekly guide can help your people prepare for worship by helping them become familiar with the new songs. See *Preparing Your Congregation for Worship* later in this book.

> Are you introducing new songs in a way that will "take hold" in the hearts of your congregation? What changes do you need to make?

SONG LISTS FOR PLANNING WORSHIP

Songs are a significant part of your church's worship. They give your congregation a voice to their worship and praise; songs are vital to building disciples. People worship best with songs they know.

In years past, people used their hymnal as their song list in planning worship. Pretty much everything your congregation sang came from that hymnal. But today, we use songs from hymnals, other songbooks, various internet sources, locally written songs, etc. Keeping up with our congregation's repertoire can be challenging.

Some people plan worship by choosing songs out of their heads. Perhaps the prompting comes from something heard on the radio this week or just a song from the past that is remembered. This overlooks many songs that may be better choices for your congregation this week.

Some worship planners have a list that includes every song their congregation has sung. It probably has well more than 200 songs on that list. While that can work fine with an older, established congregation, this becomes an immense problem if your church is experiencing growth with people who did not grow up in the church singing these songs or if your church wants to position itself to reach and disciple people in your community. **Having an extensive song list means that new people rarely know the songs you sing, preventing them from participating fully in worship.**

People using Planning Center, WorshipPlanning.com, or other online planning applications can use the list of songs in that application to plan. It can become a list of 200+ songs if you are not curating and refining it somehow. For these people, I encourage using the spreadsheet ideas I will describe below as a tool for your planning application.

This system, I believe, will help worship leaders carefully curate a master song list for worship planning that will engage their people in worship and help new believers quickly find a voice for their praise and worship.

You will also find some specialized tools I have created to help you on the journey.

> **If you have a list of songs you use in planning, how many songs are on the list? Do you ever remove songs from the list, or does it just get larger every year? How do you determine how many songs should be on your list?**

WHY IMPLEMENT THE SYSTEM?

Having too many songs on your list leads to minimal repetition of songs and the likelihood, in many cases, that many in your congregation will not know the songs you are using in worship.

Unfamiliarity with the songs breeds a lack of active participation in worship and leads your people to become spectators.

> **The size of your master song list can dramatically affect worship in your church.**

Let's think about the size of your song list. If your list has over 200 songs and your church usually sings four songs weekly in worship, then you would never repeat a song in a year if you sing all the songs! That may work if your church is made up of people who have been a part of your particular church for decades or if you are using only older, mainline hymns for a congregation of veteran church attendees.

But what if your church is growing and seeing people come to faith regularly? Perhaps you have a good number of visitors each week. Will these people who did not grow up in the church know your music? NOT LIKELY!

> **If your church is growing and reaching people, you must have a reasonable level of repetition of songs for people to sing songs they know and therefore participate in worship.**

We must also consider that the average church attendee does not worship at your church every week. Even if they attend every other week on average, that dramatically impacts the number of times they encounter a particular song on your master song list. (If you sing a song four times in a year and they only attend half of the time, they might sing it twice.)

Too many songs on your song list will make it difficult for the congregation to worship.

If you want to help your congregation really sing by assisting them in singing songs they know, you **MUST LIMIT THE SIZE OF YOUR MASTER SONG LIST.**

> **A master song list should be long enough to provide variety for your congregation yet short enough to provide familiarity.**

FOUR TYPES OF SONGS YOU WILL USE ON YOUR SONG LIST

To ensure variety for my congregation, I classify songs on my list in one of four ways, as described below. You may find that different classifications work better for your setting.

1. Hymns

I probably don't need much explanation here. The great hymns that have survived the test of time are necessary to help us connect with our heritage, and they are the musical heart language of some generations of worshippers in our congregation. Modern hymns, such as those coming from the Getty or Sovereign Grace camps, are not included in this category. For the sake of the assignment, we can say that hymns are written before the 1980s.

2. Classic worship songs

These are those timeless worship songs that have lingered with us. So many new songs are popular for a few months to a few years — then they burn out and are rarely used again. Classics have stood the test of time and, when brought out in the service once again, can be embraced as a great expression of worship for the congregation. Think of songs like *Shout to the Lord*, *Blessed Be Your Name*, or *How Great Is Our God*. My arbitrary date assignment would be around 1980 to no less than 15 years old. For people in your congregation who have attended church for several years, these classics will probably be well-known the first week you use them.

3. Modern worship songs

These are the songs written in the last 15 years. For some churches, you may want to make that time period much less. These can include many styles of songs, but they all are more modern expressions of our faith, representing the move of God in more current times. As mentioned before, modern hymns would also fall under this category.

4. New songs

These are songs that are new to your congregation. They can come from any of the previous three categories, but they generally represent a modern worship song. These songs will need to be repeated many times at first to gain familiarity and become part of your congregation's worship vocabulary.

NOTE: You may desire to add another category or vary these. Grasping the overall concept is essential, but you certainly have the freedom to fit it into the way that best serves your congregation.

> **Remember that a song list that is too big or too small may negatively impact your church's expression of worship each week.**

THREE DISTINCT SONG LIST CATEGORIES THAT SHOULD BE A PART OF YOUR MASTER SONG LIST

Creating three lists will help you in your planning. One list will be the list you plan from. One will be a list that you keep new songs you will be systematically introducing to the church, and finally, there is a list to keep retired songs that may come back to your primary list in the future. Below are the descriptions of the three lists:

1. Current songs

This is the list that you use to plan worship. This list is carefully curated with the correct number and types of songs, as we will discuss in a moment.

2. Under consideration songs

This is your list of songs that have met all the requirements for a new song that you will eventually introduce to your congregation. These have been carefully filtered musically and textually, as discussed earlier. Songs on this list will likely end up on the current song list in the future.

3. Retired songs

When you remove a song from the current song list, you can place it on the retired song list unless you feel it does not warrant using it again in the future. This list can grow to be very large in the future.

> **Don't keep using good songs when you can focus on the great songs for your congregation.**

FORMATTING YOUR MASTER SONG LIST

I enter all the information in a spreadsheet that can be sorted for help in planning worship. I have templates available at WorshipMinistryGuidebook.com to help with this process. I like including specific details on each song to help me plan worship. Here are some suggestions. The information marked with asterisks is the most important.

1. ***Song Title**

2. ***Key 1** — This should be a congregationally-friendly key and include the final key if the arrangement changes keys. The ability to sort by keys is extremely important in planning seamless worship song sets that flow well, as you will see in a later lesson.

3. **Key 2** (if applicable) — This should be a congregationally-friendly key and include the final key if the arrangement changes keys.

4. **Source** — You may want to note where the arrangement originates (LifeWayWorship, PraiseCharts, etc.).

5. ***Category** — Choose the appropriate song type from the drop-down selection.

6. **Tempo #** — What is the metronomic setting for the piece?

7. **Tempo** — Choose fast, medium, or slow from the drop-down selection.

8. **Meter** — Choose the correct time signature from the drop-down selection.

I have created some online tools to help you determine the number of songs you need on your song list and ways to utilize that list. You can find the resources, as well as sample song lists, at WorshipMinistryGuidebook.com.

OTHER OPTIONS FOR PRODUCING YOUR SONG LIST

Online worship planning applications can also handle lists. Still, I have found that having a separate list (spreadsheet), as I described, is easier to manage and interact with. You can additionally update your song lists in your online apps to make them work together better.

CLOSING THOUGHTS ON SONG LISTS

I encourage those with a very high number of songs on their list to consider the reasoning in this writing and determine if you want to get your list in a better position to help your congregation really worship with songs they know well.

If your congregation is an older congregation made up of people that have been attending church all their life and you have very few people that are not longtime attendees, then perhaps a very large list works well for you.

If you want to connect with those outside of that description, I believe your list needs to be pared down considerably.

Developing a song list takes time, but pays great dividends in worship planning and helping your congregation engage in transformational worship. Make it a priority to set aside time soon to develop your song list if you do not have one, or to determine needed changes in an existing list.

WORSHIP TRANSITIONS

The following section gives practical help in designing a worship service with a strong element of free-flowing praise, yet with the convergence of other worship formats. Of particular interest is the ability to bring an element of direction and theme within a model of free-flowing praise within the constraints and limitations of a local church's worship time. Musical considerations are critical in linking together songs in extended times of singing. Textual and thematic links are important in providing direction and flow to a service and reinforcing the pastor's message. Before we consider the whole concept of planning the worship experience, it is best to understand how songs effectively link together to provide a seamless flow in worship. I have expanded on some of these ideas, with permission, from Don Chapman of WorshipIdeas.com.[65]

LINKING WORSHIP SONGS: MUSICAL CONSIDERATIONS

First, we consider ways to connect songs musically so that they flow seamlessly from one to another. This offsets the awkward and disjointed practice that usually occurs of finishing a song and then having an awkward filler as you get the next song ready to go. In musically linking songs, the second song flows out of the first, creating a sense of journey and connection. There are three primary methods that we will use to link songs together in worship:

INTRO OVERLAP

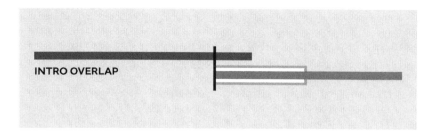

In the ***intro overlap*** method, as the last note of the first song is sung, the introduction to the second song begins underneath. The new song's feel, and perhaps a change of tempo, take over precisely at that point, drawing the congregation into the second song. This method requires the last chord of the first song and the first chord of the second song to be the same, so usually, this method works for two songs in the same key.

SHORT GAP

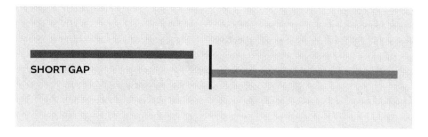

In the ***short gap*** method, the first song ends, and the second song begins after a very brief moment, just enough to "clear the air." This method best connects songs a whole or half step apart and songs where the second song is a spontaneous response to the first.

NO BREAK

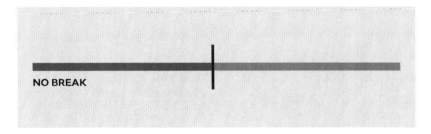

The *no break* method joins the two songs, with one song beginning as the other ends. The beat constantly continues without a break. Freedom comes in determining the length (or existence) of outros and intros to craft the amount of instrumental bridging between the sung portions of the two songs. This method works for songs in the same key or a fourth or fifth apart.

Below you will find examples of ways to connect songs in smooth transitions divided by key relationships. While mastering this skill will take work, it will provide great moments fo worship.

KEY RELATIONSHIPS

Songs in the same key and same meter will almost always work well together.

If the tempos are the same, begin the introduction of the second song on the last sung note of the previous song. *(intro overlap)*

Suppose **the tempos of the songs are not the same.** In that case, you can creatively add a tag, extra chorus, etc., to the end of the first song at the second song's tempo, if appropriate, then move to the second song by **beginning the introduction of the second song on the last sung note of the previous song.** *(intro overlap)*

Segue directly, singing the next song after a very brief pause. This may work well where the tempos are pretty different to provide just enough time over a sustained chord to have a drummer count off the new beat. This also works very well with the planned spontaneity approach described later in this section. *(short gap)*

Segue directly, singing the next song at the completion of the first song. This requires you to go quickly into the next song. If it seems too rushed, consider using the following connection idea. *(no break)*

Play an extra measure or two of "filler" between the two songs as you segue directly into singing the second song. *(no break)*

Use your creativity to craft a smooth flow as to how many measures to end the first song and how many measures to introduce the second song. You can prepare a musical interlude of enough time for a key passage of Scripture, set a new feel, or move very quickly into the next song, depending on what you want to accomplish.

> ### Songs in a key, a half or a whole step apart, work nicely together.

Note: It is generally best to move up in keys, not down.

It is almost always best to **end one song and immediately**

start the following introduction in the higher key. *(short gap)*

At times, **using the dominant seventh chord of the second song** is effective in leading you to the new key. An example going from Bb to C: Bb > F/G (IV/V in new key) > G7 (V7 in new key) > C *(no gap)*

Modulate inside the first song to sing a verse, chorus, or bridge a half or a whole step higher (in the same key as the second song), then use one of the methods for joining songs in the same key. *(intro overlap)*

> **Moving up a fourth or a fifth works nicely, too.**

Note: this transition, moving up a fourth or a fifth, is probably the best sounding to the ears other than a transition going to a song in the same key. For instance, if you are in the key of C and you are going to a song in the key of F (IV) or G (V), it will sound correct to the ear as you move to the new song since the F (or G) major chord was a part of the song in C. It provides a beautiful transition to a song in another key.

Begin the introduction of the second song directly after ending the previous song if the tempo is the same. *(no break)*

Begin the introduction of the second song after a very brief pause if the tempo of one song is different from the others. *(short gap)*

Segue directly, singing the next song after the first or after a brief pause. NOTE: The second song is in a new key. You MUST be confident of the first note of the second song without needing instrumental aid. This is another connection idea for planned spontaneity. *(short gap)*

Note that many contemporary worship songs end on the IV chord. When the song ends on the IV chord, **you can go straight to the vocals of the second song**, a fourth above in many cases, without any introduction to establish the new key. *(short gap)*

PLANNED SPONTANEITY

I use this expression to describe a planned connection between two songs where it seems, as you end the first song, as though you've suddenly thought of a second song that would be a great response to the first. Then, you lead directly into singing it. The spontaneous second song would often begin with very little instrumentation — perhaps just keyboard pads. The song could then build as you move forward. Planned spontaneity works best between songs in the same key, but it also works nicely in settings such as the above example in which a song that ends on the IV chord goes to a song in a key a fourth higher. The critical part, in this case, is that the worship leader must know what note to begin on and get the new key in mind immediately since there is no introduction to establish the key. This effect can be very powerful in worship. *(short gap)*

MOVING TO A NON-SIMPLE KEY

Sometimes you may have to use two songs in succession that don't have simple key transitions. It is often best in these situations to have a brief break between songs for prayer, Scripture reading, or another worship element. It would be appropriate for one or more musicians to begin playing incidental music quietly in the new key, following a pause to "clear the air" of the first key.

CHART OF MAJOR KEY RELATIONSHIPS FOR SIMPLE TRANSITIONS

Use this chart to quickly determine the five keys a second song may be in to form a seamless transition between two pieces. Remember that one song may go to another in the same key, a half-step or whole step above, or up a fourth or fifth. In general, I find staying in the same key or moving up a fourth or fifth makes the smoothest transitions.

KEY	UP 1/2 STEP	UP WHOLE STEP	UP FOURTH	UP FIFTH
A	Bb/A#	B	D	E
Bb/A#	B	C	Eb/D#	F
B	C	Db/C#	E	F#/Gb
C	Db/C#	D	F	G
Db/C#	D	Eb/D#	F#/Gb	Ab/G#
D	Eb/D#	E	G	A
Eb/D#	E	F	Ab/G#	Bb/A#
E	F	F#/Gb	A	B
F	F#/Gb	G	Bb/A#	C
F#/Gb	G	Ab/G#	B	Dd/C#
G	Ab/G#	A	C	D
Ab/G#	A	Bb/A#	Db/C#	Eb/D#

Remember key relationships between songs
in worship. Always know where you are and
where you are going so you will know what note is
ahead and not have to wait on the instrumentalists
to lead you in establishing the song.

Are successive songs in your worship sets
usually disjointed, lacking a smooth flow
from one to another? What actions can
you take to overcome this problem?

LINKING WORSHIP SONGS: TEXTUAL CONSIDERATIONS

In addition to the key relationships, you can make connections between songs through the text. When you can utilize a textual connection AND a musical connection, you create a much more powerful transition. Consider these additional ways to link songs.:

TEXT LINK

Look at the lyrics and see if any key words or phrases suggest another song. Consider all verses of a song as well as the possibilities of starting with a chorus, bridge, or phrase of a song. Switching verses of a song can be done to assist with linking texts as long as it still makes sense in that order. You could finish the song, *Agnus Dei* (in A), and then move to *Worthy Is the Lamb* (also in A) with a no break connection going into the chorus of *Worthy Is the Lamb*. The connecting text link is the phrase, "Worthy is the Lamb."

Additionally, we could begin a set with *You Are My King* and end with the lyrics "You are my King." We would then go directly to the first line of *How Great Is Our God*, "The splendor of the King." At the end of the chorus of *How Great is Our God*, we would go directly into the chorus of *How Great Thou Art*, singing, "Then sings my soul, my Savior God to Thee, how great Thou art …"

Here's another example: Begin with *Open the Eyes of My Heart* (in E). End with the section saying, "Holy, holy, holy, I want to see You." Then go directly into the song, *We Fall Down* (in E going to F), but begin with the chorus: "And we cry holy, holy, holy, is the Lamb." We could then segue into *Holy, Holy, Holy*. We could use the PraiseCharts arrangement that begins in the key of C and modulates twice to arrive in the key of D. When we complete that song, we could go directly into *Revelation Song* (key of D). We have now accomplished a set of music linking four songs by text and key!

Open the Eyes of My Heart (E) > *We Fall Down* (E-F) > *Holy, Holy, Holy* (C-D) > *Revelation Song* (D)

THEMATIC LINK

Songs can link together based solely on their themes. Topical indexes are great places to find songs of similar themes. Selecting two or more songs on the topic of grace, for instance, would provide this type of link. Additionally, it would be best if you strived to connect the songs with key relationships for smoother transitions.

RESPONSE LINK

As you finish singing a song, think: "Where do I naturally want to go next? How do I want to respond?" Example: You have just finished singing *Goodness of God*. The instrumentalists sustain the final A chord. The worship leader begins to sing the chorus of "God, you're so good" (remaining in the key of A) as a quiet, heartfelt response to the previous song. **This is an example of a response link that is a planned spontaneity moment using the short gap method connecting two songs in the same key.**

You will find more examples, including video examples, of transitions at WorshipMinistryGuidebook.com.

> **Take some time to create a few song transitions using these methods.**

NON-MUSICAL ELEMENTS OF WORSHIP

As worship planners, we must consider much more than just great songs in our worship plans. Think about using prayers, Bible reading, teachings, testimonies, Lord's Supper, baptism, videos, creeds/other readings, monologues, and other creative arts. Not only will this engage the giftedness of more of your church members, but it will also engage the hearts of your people in ways that music alone cannot do. Open your mind and imagination to ways to engage your congregation in worship by breaking out of the box of doing things the same way each week. We will talk more about this as we get into planning the worship service.

ROLE OF PRESENTATIONAL/ REPRESENTATIONAL MUSIC

While the primary role of the church choir and other ensembles is to lead and engage the congregation in singing their praises, there is a place for a more *presentational* or *representational* function in our times of gathered worship. Many churches have eliminated special music, since it can seem more of a performance, spectator-creating element of the worship service. While that can be true in many cases, I believe there is still a place for presentational music in the service.

The best description of the role of presentational music in the church I have seen comes from Constance Cherry's book, *The Music Architect: Blueprints for Engaging Worshippers in Song*:

> *Presentational music is music that is prepared in advance by one or more musicians to be presented on behalf of other worshippers for the glory of God. Most of the music offered in worship should be communally rendered. This practice is good and right. However, there is a place for music that is offered representatively. In many churches presentational music, sometimes referred to as "special music," has been eliminated in favor of congregational song exclusively. Yet presentational music has a role in communal worship as long as the emphasis remains predominantly on congregational singing.* **Perhaps a better term is "representational music" — songs or instrumental pieces that are prepared by qualified members of the community and then offered on behalf of the community, which represents the voices of the whole.** *It is understood that such music serves the same functions in worship as other songs sung by the group (proclamation, prayer, exhortation, etc.) but is simply voiced*

by prepared members. It is also understood at the same time to be edifying to one's fellow worshippers, inspiring them in their own offerings of praise and prayer. Have you ever heard someone eloquently say something and thought, "I wish I could have put it that way"? That experience is in keeping with presentational music. Presentational music should never be viewed as performance music — something presented primarily for the enjoyment of others — though it certainly may be enjoyed. Instead, it must be viewed as representative music that speaks in order to enrich, enable and inspire their worship of God.[66]

Cherry references James White in his summary of the role of the choir (or another ensemble) in worship as having three possible functions:

1. To sing *to* the congregation by sharing in the ministry of word;
2. To sing *for* the congregation in the offering of beauty, and
3. To sing *with* the congregation in leading congregational song [67]

I believe presentational music can still have a place in gathered worship if utilized with the correct heart and understanding. In my example of God's call on my life, describing the two churches in Texas, you can see how a choir's presentational song can be a profound time of worship for the congregants.

If your church has a choir, do you need to help them grasp their functions and help them be more of a worship catalyst?

THE WORSHIP PLANNING TEAM

Worship planning takes on a greater dimension when you bring others into the planning process. A Worship Planning Team (WPT) or Creative Worship Arts Team is of great value.

Creating a Worship Planning Team will accomplish a few things:

1. It will provide an excellent platform for planning worship services drawing from people with various strengths and talents.
2. It will aid the current worship leader, who perhaps has previously led only traditional worship, to plan and lead the new form of worship.
3. It will take advantage of the great storehouse of creative talents in the worship arts that may not be currently utilized.
4. It will provide multisensory worship experiences for your congregation.
5. It will diffuse any pushback to an entire team rather than one person.

THE CONCEPT

I will present a scenario I used in a church that yielded great results. Adapt these ideas to meet the needs of your congregation and the people you identify as potential team members.

The Worship Leadership Team would meet weekly to plan corporate worship times. **The members represent many disciplines of the arts**, such as drama, graphics, video, photography, interpretive movement, and art. There would also be **additional people with creative abilities** and **a couple of musicians**. Ideally, **the senior pastor** will also meet with the team (if not in person, he will need to send detailed information). He can share his ideas concerning upcoming sermons or special directions he would like to see incorporated into worship.

The team would take this information and begin brainstorming ways to **impact the congregation in worship by engaging the senses**. For instance, the person with drama strength on the team may conceptualize a powerful way to relay the message through drama. Others may think of a way to engage the congregation through images on screen or poetry or changing the worship space. For instance, if the team determines that in a service four weeks from now, we will have a drama, utilize a powerful graphic on the cover of the bulletin, and use a video from another source, then the drama director would have the script written, enlist the team, and prepare the drama for the service. The graphic people would prepare their work. Someone would also be responsible for securing the video.

The worship leader/pastor would orchestrate all of these elements into the worship service for the day. Some WPTs plan every detail of the service, including the music. Others leave some of those details to the worship leader.

Utilizing such an approach will engage people with creative abilities beyond just musicians to use their gifts for God's glory and the congregation's good. **Discover whom God has placed in your church that you can involve in this way, and help them fulfill a calling on their lives to use their gifts to build up the church.**

STEPS TO CREATING A FUNCTIONING TEAM

1. **Identify key members with varying talents in the worship arts and enlist them to serve on the team.**

2. **Schedule a retreat to cast vision and begin to work together.** This is a real key. Help the team members understand their purpose and see how the group works together. Great synergy can result!

3. **Plan the first four worship services beginning with the target launch date.** The pastor will need to relay sermon information for those four weeks to the team and preferably talk through what he hopes to accomplish each week.

4. **Develop teams for various disciplines**—drama, interpretive movement, art, video, etc. You might conduct an interest survey to determine the talents of church members in the worship arts.

> Are there people in your church with creative gifts that can help your gathered worship times to be more meaningful and impactful?

BALANCING SPIRIT AND TRUTH

We are all familiar with Jesus's response to the woman at the well: *Yet a time is coming and has now come when the true worshippers will worship the Father in spirit and truth, for they are the kind of worshippers the Father seeks. God is spirit, and his worshippers must worship in spirit and in truth.* John 4:23-24, NIV

How should we look at these contrasting terms of spirit and truth? Consider these ways of looking at spirit and truth: heart vs. mind; emotions vs. intellect; nonverbal vs. verbal; unpredictable vs. predictable; symbolic and creative vs. orderly and oriented. [68]

Some churches lean to the spirit side. Worship is generally spontaneous and Spirit-led. Services tend to be more physical and emotional. **Other segments of the church lean to the truth side.** Here worship is more orderly and structured. Each tradition has great values.

But Jesus said that true worshippers must worship in spirit and truth, not one or the other. Both traditions are missing the mark of worship as God intends it to be. If our services are steeped in truth, we need to blend more spirit into our worship times.

I have attended church services that lean strongly to the spirit side; there is a lot of spontaneity and little structure. In these churches, there may be no planned order of worship. Worship flows from one element to the other as the leader senses the movement of the Spirit. People in this tradition will often look at the structure of the "truth" churches and feel that they have shut out the ability of the Holy Spirit to work in the service. Those more structured churches often feel the "spirit" churches are not providing well for their congregants by not carefully planning the worship experience to meet their discipleship and worship needs.

Both camps fall short too often.

Today, churches often schedule their services to the minute for each element of worship. This song is allotted 5 minutes and 30 seconds; this prayer is limited to two minutes; the video will run 2:15, etc. **But what happens when God shows up in an unexplained way?** If our services are programmed to the second in Ableton and Planning Center, and our in-ear guide tells us the song is ending, what do we do if suddenly the altar is filling up with people pouring their hearts out to God in the middle of a song?

The answer is to **plan thoroughly and be ready to flex**. As we pray and lean on God in the planning process, He can certainly guide the plans as He desires. Then, as we lead in worship, we must always be aware of what is happening among the people. Is God moving in a way that our plan can be a barrier? If so, what change do I need to make?

I was in a service a few years ago where a song was planned as intro, verse, chorus, verse, chorus, bridge, chorus, chorus, tag, and outro. On the final two choruses, people spontaneously came to the altar and cried out to God. Since the song was running with backing tracks, the worship leader let the music end as planned, and they moved directly into a time of announcements even while the people were still at the altar. This was incredibly insensitive and exhibited poor leadership and a lack of following the Spirit's prompting.

We need structure and plans under the guidance of the Holy Spirit, but we also need the flexibility to change as we sense the need. It might mean extending a song, adding another song, moving to a time of silence, a season of prayer, or something else. At those special times, **don't let the ball and chain of your worship plan hinder what is happening in the people's hearts.**

Being flexible and spontaneous may be difficult for your team. This is something you need to try out regularly in rehearsals. Go off the plan without anyone knowing and see how people react. Talk about how everyone can get more comfortable with spontaneity. The more you "rehearse" these times of spontaneity, the more comfortable your band, singers, and technicians will be when it happens in worship.

When I was leading worship at a church where everyone needed written out music for anything we did (as opposed to the ability to play by ear easily), I would often have several additional songs that were well-known ready to go each week if we needed to move to another song. The person operating the lyric slides also had those songs prepared if needed. It provided several additional options for spontaneity if we felt another song was needed at some time. If you are using technology such as backing tracks, the person operating those tracks should know how to repeat sections or end a song early as well as jump to a song not in the original plan.

Realize, too, in these times of spontaneity, you may not need to move to a new song or continue into another piece. As I mentioned before, it might instead mean we should move to a time of silence, a season of prayer, or something else.

Ask God to make you and your team flexible to His moving in your services. Then, keep your spiritual eyes open at all times to what is happening in worship. Don't get so caught up in the fantastic plan you are implementing in worship that you can't see what God is doing.

> **We should never make production
> more important than presence.**

In his book, Desiring God, John Piper writes:

> *Worship must be vital and real in the heart, and worship must rest on a true perception of God. There must be spirit and there must be truth. … Truth without emotion produces dead orthodoxy and a church full (or half-full) of artificial admirers.*

... On the other hand, emotion without truth produces empty frenzy and cultivates shallow people who refuse the discipline of rigorous thought. But true worship comes from people who are deeply emotional and who love deep and sound doctrine. Strong affections for God rooted in truth are the bone and marrow of biblical worship.[69]

Where you have all truth and no spirit, the people tend to dry up

Where you have all spirit and no truth, the people tend to blow up

Where you have truth and spirit, the people tend to grow up.[70]

> **What does this look like in the practicality of worship? In what ways do you need to prepare for the spontaneous in worship with your team?**

PLANNING THE WORSHIP SERVICE

It has taken quite a while to get to this section of the book. Before we can be entrusted to the planning of the service, we must understand the foundational aspects of worship discussed in chapters one and two. Additionally, the concepts presented in this chapter are the building blocks to designing a worship service that will engage your congregation in worship.

While the Bible does not clearly prescribe what the worship service should look like, there is guidance for our quest. Steven

Brooks compiles the New Testament "essentials" for corporate worship:

1. Reading the Word (1 Tim 4:13–15)
2. Preaching (Acts 2:42; 1 Tim 4:13; 2 Tim 3:15–17; 4:2)
3. Praying (1 Tim 2:1; 1 Cor 14:16; Heb 4:16; cf. Acts 1:14; 2:1; 4:24, 32)
4. Singing (Eph 5:19; Col 3:16; Rev 5:9–13; 15:3, 4)
5. Regularly observing baptism (Matt 28:19, 20; cf. Acts 2:41; 8:12, 36–38; 9:18) and the Lord's Supper (Acts 2:42; 1 Cor 11:24–30)
6. Regularly giving to the work of the Word (1 Cor 16:2; 2 Cor 9:7)[71]

As worship planners, we need to be faithful in including all of these in our times of gathered worship.

> **As worship leaders/planners, we need to identify and eliminate as many distractions as possible so that we can create an environment that helps people to connect with God.**

As we begin the process of planning worship, we need to prayerfully ask God to guide us in the planning, to help us choose the best songs for that day, to be drawn to the other elements of worship to be used in the service, and to set an atmosphere to help people experience God in worship.

In keeping with the convergence worship format, we want to consider pulling the best of liturgical and thematic worship while keeping a free-flowing praise fluidness to the service, eliminating awkward, disjointed moments (unless the Spirit leads into a more "messy" experience).

View the worship service as an experience from the beginning to the end, employing music, the arts, testimony, Scripture, prayers, ministry times, and more to help the congregation experience God in worship.

STEPS TO WORSHIP PLANNING

In the remainder of this chapter and the next chapter, I intend to present **a practical guide to help you move a worship service from conception to implementation**, looking closely at several areas. This section will deal with the planning of the service, and the next chapter will look at how to implement the plan in preparing for worship.

For a worship leader, planning, rehearsing, and implementing the worship service are primary tasks. All the preparation for the worship service grows out of the worship plan you create. Here are some steps to creating this plan:

MEET WITH THE PASTOR

In planning worship, it can be much more meaningful for some of the non-sermonic parts of the service to support the sermon material. We talked about this in relation to the thematic format of worship. It can be very meaningful if one or two service elements connect with the sermon, particularly if you have any presentational music. Further, if you utilize a worship leadership team and need to prepare drama, videos, readings, etc., several weeks may be required for preparation. For this reason, beginning with sermon information several weeks ahead will significantly facilitate the planning process since some elements of worship take more time to prepare (such as presentational music like choir selections, locally-created videos, drama, etc.). Pastors should see the great benefit of providing that information weeks ahead as the times of corporate worship become more engaging and meaningful. Pastors, give your worship leader sermon information minimally two months ahead, if possible. Three months or more is a hallelujah goal!

I realize that it is just a dream for many worship leaders to receive sermon information weeks ahead of time. Many I talk with have yet to get advanced notice of sermon information. I would encourage you to speak with your pastor about some of the benefits of being able to strengthen the message and see if he would be willing to work out advanced notice. If not, do not dismay; you can still create powerful worship services without the thematic connection.

CHOOSE THE CHOIR SONGS AND OTHER PRESENTATIONAL MUSIC

Preparing a choir, ensemble, or soloist is best done with advance notice. I prefer beginning a new choir anthem at least 6-8 weeks ahead of the target Sunday. Meditate on the sermon information your pastor has provided and prayerfully search for presentational music that will support the direction of the message. Of course, sometimes you will not make that connection, or you will prefer to go a different direction. Still, you need to plan out the presentational music 6-8 weeks ahead for appropriate preparation that will yield excellence (more later when we discuss choirs).

I strongly recommend using a worship planning tool to help you stay organized and streamline your work. I discovered that a tool like Planning Center or WorshipPlanning.com will revolutionize your life in planning worship and working the plan from conception to "delivery." In it, you can:

- plan all worship services,
- maintain your song library that will share all files with musicians assigned to a service for their preparation,
- manage your worship teams,
- schedule your volunteers, including tech teams, and
- communicate with everyone as needed.

Do you see how amazing this is to streamline your work? All your resources are uploaded to the application so that you merely drop in the songs and other elements of worship in the planning process. Then you assign your teams and send out a notification that they can respond to. They have full access to the songs, service order, notes, mp3s, prep information, and much more—it gives them everything they need to prepare for rehearsal successfully.

WORSHIP PLANNING TOOLS

Before I began using an online worship planning application, I used Microsoft Word, Excel, email, Dropbox or Google Drive, and a variety of other great applications. No monthly subscriptions were assessed using these options as long as you could maintain your files in the free cloud storage quota, but there was a significantly increased workload. I will discuss how to utilize these different technologies in the following pages.

Here's the bottom line: the only advantage I found in the variety of applications was that I did not need to make a further financial investment to do this work. But finding all I need in one place is a great time saver and organizational wonder. With one of the online applications, at this stage, I enter all the sermon information, notes, possible creative elements, possible presentational music ideas, and much more. It then provides a canvas upon which I can plan the worship service.

CONSIDER APPROPRIATE CONGREGATIONAL SONGS FROM YOUR SONG LIST.

Next, you should select possible songs from your song list to use in the service. As you prayerfully consider the sermon information, think of a song or two that may fit that well, if appropriate. As you select the songs, include the congregationally-friendly keys for each piece to help you in a later stage of planning. Think about musical and textual linking in sets of two or more songs. As you select songs:

- Spend some time praising the attributes of God.
- Have songs that focus on prayer, confession, celebration, and more.
- Choose songs that help your congregation voice their worship.

DISCOVER CREATIVE ELEMENTS OF WORSHIP.

What are some ways that you can make this service become more alive for the church? Consider videos, drama, dance, readings, art, and other creative arts. There are hundreds of resources online that are linked at WorshipMinistryGuidebook. com. You can also utilize creative people in your church to create and provide these elements for worship, as was discussed with the worship planning team. Remember that many of these elements will need several weeks of prep time.

BE AWARE OF SPECIAL INCLUSIONS IN THE SERVICE.

On a given Sunday, you may have the Lord's Supper, baptism, parent-child dedication, graduate recognition, or other special observances. These all can take a significant portion of the service. Some of these things should be central in your worship rather than a service tag-on. Treat them accordingly.

DESIGN A SEQUENCE OF EVENTS.

Now that you have gathered various worship elements, you will begin to flesh out the service fully. The order in which each part (song, prayer, Bible reading, creative element, etc.) is placed must be carefully considered and ordered logically and progressively. Keep in mind the key relationships of the songs you have selected to ensure smooth transitions. **The worship event should be a logical, unfolding drama, not a selection of loosely strung items.**

While not necessary, a common practice is to begin with faster praise-themed congregational worship songs and work towards quieter, more intimate worship music later in the service. This follows an Old Testament model of worship in the temple and makes sense in another way; when people are just arriving for worship, they are often not ready to be intimately involved in worship at the outset but need some time to focus their minds and hearts toward God. A song that helps gather people and their affections is a good start.

We do not want to be so predictable that we utilize the same service order every week along with the same progression of songs. We want to constantly be awakening people's imaginations as we declare the majesty of our God in worship. Try not to get in a rut of worship planning. Be creative. Change things up.

Realize that announcements or introductions of guests interfere with the flow of worship. Offload announcements to videos and digital communication, including social media channels, printed sheets, etc. Make only the most important, necessary announcements at the beginning or end of the service so worship flow is not adversely affected.

CREATE MUSICAL SEGUES AND TRANSITIONS.

Build musical bridges between songs (see the section *Linking Worship Songs*). It is best to keep a continual flow between songs in a set. If you stop a song abruptly, the progression will stop and have to start all over again. There are times when pausing or waiting is appropriate; however, these transitions should be rare. Also, plan transitions between each element of the service. For instance, determine how you will move from an opening song to a prayer time to another song. Examples are given in the sample service at WorshipMinistryGuidebook.com.

CHECK THE CONTENT AND FLOW.

You now have a nearly final worship service. Take some time to think through the whole worship flow. Consider how suitable each element is that you have included. Take a break and look at the flow with fresh eyes sometime later. Ask yourself, "How will I move from that item to the next?" "Should I place that item earlier or later into the service?" "Are there too many new songs (should be no more than one)?" "Is there a wide variety of Scripture passages and other elements to which the whole congregation will relate?" These kinds of questions will help you fix potential weaknesses. You will also find it helpful to run through any musical transitions to check whether they will work. Make adjustments sooner rather than later.

EVALUATE FOR PARTICIPATION.

The final step is to evaluate your service plan according to the level of participation that will be required of the worshipper. Remember that worship is not a spectator sport but a participatory event in which each person contributes as fully as possible. Spend some time working through the plan to identify all the ways in which people will participate. Take each worship element and ask yourself how you could use it to facilitate congregational participation. It will involve more preparation to have others read, share or act, but this is necessary for worship to be a truly participatory event.

THROUGHOUT THE PROCESS, COLLABORATE WITH THE PASTOR.

More than two weeks out, I want to have a rough draft of the service to share with the pastor. Ideally, you will communicate along the way as the service comes together. At this time, share what you have designed to be the final plan to get a green light or make a modification before publishing to the rest of your team.

FINALIZE THE SERVICE TWO WEEKS OUT.

For some people, your practice may be to have the services completed a few days before Sunday (or even Saturday night!). Still, we need more time to get all the preparation done and the resources ready for your team to have ample time to practice before rehearsals.

As I mentioned, It is best to have your planning done a couple of weeks out so that all the preparation can fall into place. Many of the creative elements (if produced in-house) and the presentational music need to be planned at least 6-8 weeks ahead for best results. By two weeks out, you will have added congregational music and other elements and developed the best flow for the order of worship. Once that is completed, you can send out a communication to the people scheduled for that service, letting them know their resources are ready so that they can begin preparing.

Now you have a plan in place, and the resources are prepared. In the next chapter, we will look at how to implement this plan by preparing your choir, vocal team, band, tech team, congregation, and yourself.

> **Has your worship planning been haphazard? Do you need to be more intentional in designing this weekly event that will disciple your people and give them appropriate expressions of worship?**

Preparing for Worship

I have had the wonderful opportunity to serve as an interim worship leader in a couple of great churches in the last few years. As I dug into the leadership and administration of those ministries, I discovered that what I was doing was equivalent to the duties of a bi-vocational or part-time worship leader. I had a demanding full-time job to juggle, along with the vast responsibility of leading these worship ministries. Let me say that I have great respect for those of you serving in a bi-vocational capacity—having to navigate all those life responsibilities with limited time.

As a result of these ministry opportunities, I have been looking closely at the tasks a worship leader must do each week to plan, rehearse, and implement a worship service with excellence. In this chapter, I will present **a practical guide that can help you move a worship service from conception to implementation,** looking closely at several areas.

So many churches today are either multigenerational or seeking to be unified in their approach, so I will focus on the needed worship preparation for churches with a choir, band (which may look very different from church to church), and vocal team. You can, of course, make adaptations according to your specific situation. Every church is unique, and I think you can adapt to your setting from the principles I will outline in this chapter.

PREPARING THE CHOIR

Choirs can be a positive piece of worship transformation in the church. Even in contemporary worship styles, choirs can be an excellent catalyst for worship renewal. Sometimes, as mentioned earlier, the traditional choir needs to be repurposed into a worship-leading choir.

In the following section, I assume your choir, in addition to leading congregational music, also sings a presentational/representational song most weeks. A presentational/representational song is simply a song the choir sings alone, without the congregation—many refer to it as special music. (See the previous chapter for more information on the choir in worship.)

SCHEDULING SONGS

For a choir to sing with confidence, they need to know the song thoroughly. Spending a few minutes on a song 6-8 weeks in a row will yield far better results than trying to learn a piece in one or two rehearsals. Many songs can be memorized if given 6-8 weeks of preparation (which is a worthy goal to strive for). Of course, songs that have been presented before can be brought to readiness in less time. I usually encourage memorization the second time the song is done, when possible. Memorized singing is much more impacting to worship.

Consult the plan of the next eight to twelve weeks of sermon topics if you have those available. Also, consider any special emphases or other inclusions. Then select appropriate choir songs to use as presentational music each Sunday (assuming the choir sings weekly). If you don't have sermon information, you can still plan ahead for several weeks in order to have the songs prepared well.

Use some already known songs, if appropriate, and introduce new songs. It is vital to give your choir a steady diet of new music; they can become disengaged if you constantly repeat the old stuff. Seek to stretch them with new styles and new challenges. This will keep your rehearsals fresh and exciting for them. It is also great to include songs done earlier that the congregation may be familiar with and that you can take to a new level of musicianship and memorization.

Calendar the selected presentational songs for each worship service where the choir will sing a presentational song for the next eight or more weeks. I prefer to use a spreadsheet for this to assist in my planning.

CREATING PRACTICE TRACKS

Creating practice tracks may be technically too challenging for some of you, but you may have someone in your church who can do this for you. Many publishers are now producing these tracks for you. **Your choir will reach a higher level of excellence if you provide them with rehearsal tracks to use outside of choir rehearsals.** The time we have together weekly is precious and limited. Your choir members listening to the choir songs as they drive, work, and play significantly increases their learning of the music. This way, you can work on more musical things in rehearsal and challenge them to go beyond the norm. These resources also greatly assist with the memorization of the songs.

I post the rehearsal tracks on the worship leader website (I'll talk more about this later) and, in some cases, produce digital media (thumb drives or CDs) for every voice part to distribute (all with proper copyright licensing). I have a guide for producing practice tracks on WorshipMinistryGuidebook.com. It has detailed instructions to help you along the way.

I have had so many choir members to thank me for these practice tracks. They listen to them while going about the routines of the day. They tell me how they worship profoundly while singing along with the tracks. In providing these tracks, you not only help them learn the music, but you help them connect with the lyrics and music in private worship, so that their singing while leading corporate worship will be an overflow of their personal times of preparation.

REHEARSAL PLANNING

Once you have scheduled the songs and produced the rehearsal tracks, you need to consider rehearsal planning. As I said earlier, your choir will learn far more from rehearsing a song six weeks for 10 minutes each than rehearsing 60 minutes in one session.

Here are some guiding principles for your planning:

- **Look at your song schedule, and then plan to begin a song six to eight weeks before the week you will sing it.** This may be different from your current philosophy, but the song for the following Sunday should be completely learned and ready to go by the time you get to that final rehearsal. The song's difficulty will dictate how many weeks of work and how much time is devoted to the music each week. Some songs will need more than eight weeks to perfect. This may be an important culture change for your people.

- **When you are rehearsing songs six to eight weeks ahead, this creates a feeling that every choir rehearsal is important.** I often hear of choir members who will not come to choir rehearsal the week before they will be absent on Sunday because they feel there is no need. Very little rehearsal time should be used for the song planned for the upcoming worship service. This eliminates people not coming to the rehearsal before a service when they will be away. It also covers those who cannot be at the rehearsal before the song is sung in worship. If they attend rehearsals regularly, they will have exposure to all the music over the course of several rehearsals.

- **Songs the choir has sung before will not need as much rehearsal time. Consider memorizing the song.** You can work on reaching a higher level of excellence and/ or memorizing the familiar song. This will significantly increase the impact of the song.

- **Begin the rehearsal with a time of worship, using the congregational songs for this week, or if a new congregational song is coming soon, begin that a week or two earlier.** This allows your choir to be better prepared to lead the congregation in worship. The choir's primary task is not being a performance group but a worship-leading team––an army of praise.

- **Once you spend time on the congregational songs, have**

the choir sing through the song coming up this week. If rehearsals have gone as projected, you should only need to spend a little time on this song. At most, you should need to tweak a couple of spots.

- **It works well to then go to a new song or one that requires some hard work while the people are still fresh.**

- **Don't feel like you need to go over the entire song every week.** Feel free to concentrate on one or two sections of the song this week. Then next week, you can add another section and review the previous week's work. We often waste time just singing the song from beginning to end each week without concentrating on various portions of the song.

- **Help the choir see patterns, such as repeated sections, to aid their learning.** This is especially helpful in memorization. For instance, point out that the second chorus is identical to the first one except for the last two measures—this will help them learn and especially memorize the song. This requires us as leaders to thoroughly know the music and help them quickly learn it.

SINGING FROM MEMORY

I have worked with many choirs that do not believe they can memorize their music nor see any real value in it. Beginning with a song they know well that is uncomplicated is a great place to start. Take one section at a time, such as the chorus, and have the choir first sing it with their music, followed by singing it from memory. Move to another section that is identical (another chorus) or very similar (perhaps the harmony on this chorus is different in a few measures), help them see any differences, and then sing that section from memory. You can add a different section next week, reviewing the past week's work and putting both sections together. Soon you will have the entire anthem memorized. The process will be much faster if they have practice tracks to help them. Once they sing from memory in worship, they will experience the freedom in leading, as well as the more powerful message they relay singing unhindered by folders and sheet music.

Once your choir begins to experience singing from memory, you will find that it gets easier and that they are more open to it. As mentioned earlier, the first time you sing a song in worship, you might want to do it with music; the next time, you can spend more rehearsal time memorizing and perfecting the song. Singing from memory will pay great dividends!

REHEARSAL SHEETS

Print a single or two-sided page that the choir picks up as they come into rehearsal. This will help the rehearsal flow more smoothly and provide additional information. Include several items on the page:

- **Rehearsal order**

  I list the congregational and choral songs we will be rehearsing in the order they will be rehearsed. This way, people can get their music in order when they arrive. It's incredible how much time this saves not having people looking for the song "with the purple cover" in the middle of rehearsal—you know what I mean. It also lets your people know you have devised a plan to utilize their time well. I also include the presentation dates beside the anthem title so people can keep up with the date the song will be sung.

- **Congregational song lyrics**
  The lyrics for the songs we will sing in worship to lead the congregation are printed on this sheet. Please include the copyright information where applicable. These can make great devotional aids as the choir members take them home and meditate on the lyrics in their times of personal worship.

- **Announcements**
  Include upcoming special services, extra rehearsals, changes in rehearsal times, etc.

- **Advertise your church's worship prep website and the worship ministry's website**
  I'll share more about these tools later.

DISCIPLESHIP

Discipleship is an important part, perhaps the most crucial part of choir preparation.

A major responsibility of the worship leader is discipleship. In choral rehearsals, bring the lyrics to life. Help them understand the biblical foundations; help them connect their testimony with the testimony of the song; and help them understand what they are singing. It will make a huge difference in their presentation when they are emotionally, spiritually, and intellectually connected to the song. We often feel so pressed for time that we don't take time for this. This is a vital part of the rehearsal time, significantly impacting the choir and the congregation. As people encounter the lyrics, their singing will become more profound, and their lives will be transformed by the power of the Holy Spirit working through them. This can be done during many teachable moments throughout the rehearsal, not just at a "scheduled" time to stop singing and have a devotional. I love to stop a song in the middle of rehearsing it with a thought about what we just sang and bring the message home to the singers. After the discipleship moment, we resume singing.

In a recent rehearsal, the choir I was leading was rehearsing, *I Speak Jesus*, made popular by Charity Gayle. It is a powerful piece that communicates well. In the midst of the strong singing of the bridge, "Jesus in the darkness over ev'ry enemy, Jesus for my fam'ly, I speak the holy name: Jesus," I was overcome with emotion. Jesus is the answer to all that ails our world. He is there for us in dark times. He is there for our families through whatever we face. I stopped the rehearsal and spoke about this and then asked them to think of ways that Jesus had been there in the dark times for them—how he had broken strongholds in their lives. I asked them to thank God in prayer for these times. I asked them to share briefly with their neighbor about this. Then we sang the bridge again, with much more emotion and passion. Just connecting what we are singing to our lives makes a tremendous difference to the message we proclaim.

COMMUNICATION

Remember that communication is huge.

If you want to impact your choir and you want your choir to have the greatest impact, then communication is a must. I like to communicate with my choir members by email at least 1-2 times a week.

1. **I usually send out an email on Monday or Tuesday,** thanking them for their leadership on Sunday, making appropriate comments about the service, and encouraging them in their calling as worship leaders. I might comment on how impacting their memorized song was this past Sunday and write about comments I heard from the people in the congregation. I encourage them and always keep their mission clear before them. Also, I may give a glimpse of the coming Sunday and our mid-week rehearsal. I want the choir to know how much I love and appreciate them.

2. **I usually send another email around Thursday or Friday** with more information about Sunday and ask them to pray for each other and the services Sunday. I often point them to the online preparation for the sermon and congregational songs.

ABSENTEES

I want to reach out weekly to anyone who missed the choir rehearsal. I let them know they were missed, tell them anything they need to know about Sunday's service to be better prepared, and find out if their absence was something that I could lift up in prayer (such as sickness or family crisis). The choir is a team and a family; when one is absent, the group hurts. I want the members to know how important they are and find out if there is a particular need in their lives that is preventing their attendance.

WEBSITE FOR WORSHIP LEADERS

A website for worship leaders is an excellent investment in their success. Websites today are so simple to produce and have little cost associated with them. I love utilizing technology to aid our worship leaders in what they do. I have a password-protected website just for our church's worship leaders where I post relevant information, upcoming song YouTube videos, practice tracks (copyright-licensed), the upcoming anthem schedule, articles of interest, and more. I communicate with my choir through this site, emails, the church worship prep site (more on this in a moment), group texts, and through an online planning application.

The churches that I have served as interim as well as the NC Baptist Singers and Orchestra (NCBSO) have all benefited from such a website. The NCBSO has access to all their music in PDF form as well as listening files for every anthem. They are expected to begin working on their music prior to our first rehearsal. Additionally, I have a plugin for the website that notifies everyone in the group anytime I publish a new post. This way all communication is archived in this one place and people are notified every time there is something new for them to look at. This communication and resource tool has been invaluable to take the group to another level as worship leaders.

PREPARING THE BAND AND VOCAL TEAM

I realize, for many of you, "the band" may consist of a single pianist and no other instrumentalist. For others, you may have a full complement of instrumentalists. Some may have an orchestra as well. Every church is uniquely different. The concepts I will discuss here may be adapted and applied to whatever your reality is.

Your "vocal team" can be you and one other person, or any number of people who assist in leading the congregational worship times.

As I mentioned, my organizational life for worship preparation is almost wholly contained in an online worship planning application. This has revolutionized my life as a worship leader. Alternately, you can also use spreadsheets for worship plans, cloud drives for music storage and distribution, and email lists for contacts.

The following steps I am going to present have three ways to accomplish the task to meet whatever level of comfort and affordability of technology you have: 1) utilizing an online planning application, 2) an ALTERNATE PLAN: using other internet-based tools that have no associated costs, and 3) the OLD SCHOOL method: using no email, no cloud services, no online technologies, just in person, telephone, and physical printing/duplicating. I remember the old school days, and frankly, I do not want to go back there, but I realize this may be the best solution for some settings.

Here are the steps to preparing your band and vocal team:

ASSIGN MUSICIANS TO THE SERVICE.

Your church may have the same instrumentalists every week, or you may be blessed with several musicians who play on rotation. These ideas will help you tackle any complications of musician assignments.

All of my music personnel have online worship planning

application accounts. Once I have set up the service date and time and added some information to the service details, I can assign my musicians to that service. They are immediately sent an email asking if they can commit to being there and serving that day. I receive their responses, so I know if someone will be out and is in need of a sub, if available.

I schedule personnel several weeks out so I can make adjustments for absences with plenty of time to make those arrangements. If some players are stronger than others, knowing who is playing on a particular Sunday can aid in song selection, considering the song's difficulty and the player's ability. You can schedule your personnel without having the service fully planned yet; then, you can send out an email when the resources are ready.

Here's the ALTERNATE PLAN: If you can get all your musicians to have a Facebook account, you can create a private Facebook group just for your musicians, create an event for each worship service, and invite those you want to participate to that event. They can respond through Facebook as to their availability. You can also use this private group page for most of your communication. Alternatively, you can contact each person by text or email to check their availability.

Now, the OLD SCHOOL method: call each musician or talk with them in person to ensure they can play on a given week. Keep a notepad to record their responses.

FINALIZE YOUR WORSHIP PLAN.

As I said before, finalizing your worship plan about two weeks ahead of time is best. When I select a song for the service, I merely pull the song from my online planning application library into the service, and all the associated files come with the song. So, if I plan to do *How Great Is Our God*, my musicians can click on that song and find the specific musical score they need (whether it is a lead sheet, vocal chart, piano, chord chart, cello, or whatever). I also have an audio file they can download or listen to online to help them prepare.

Here's the ALTERNATE PLAN: Before online planning applications entered my life, I used Word or Excel to lay out the service plan. You could also use excellent free apps such as Google Docs and Sheets. I included all the needed information in the service flow for the musicians (I'll discuss that shortly) and saved it as a PDF for digital distribution. You can then use a cloud storage account, such as DropBox, Box, or Google Drive to create service folders in which you can drop all needed print and audio files for each song, the service flow, and any other support documents.

The OLD SCHOOL method is to print out the worship plan and distribute copies of it and the needed sheet music to each instrumentalist. Prepare and distribute digital media of all demos they need to hear. Don't forget the CCLI Rehearse License to cover your digital duplication license needs.

INCLUDE SONG MAPS AND OTHER NOTES FOR EACH SONG.

You need to make your plan for the song clear—will you do verse, chorus, verse, chorus, bridge, chorus, chorus, tag (VCVCBCCT), or some other plan for the song? Will you do it as written in the charts, or will you modify what is on the page somehow? Make all of this clear ahead of time. In some online applications, there is a place for a default song map that will populate in the service when you drag it in. You can also edit this. Here you make clear your intention of how the song will be done in worship. I often explain changes in the arrangement in the notes section as well. (As I mentioned, do allow this plan to change in the worship service as the Holy Spirit may lead—don't be so rigid that you can't change the plan when God is moving in a service.) Next, describe the introduction and who will play it. If you have two or more songs together in the service, outline how the band will transition between those two songs. All of this information should be entered into the notes section.

Now the ALTERNATE PLAN: In your word processor or spreadsheet, include the song map, arrangement information, and instructions about the introduction or bridge between the songs. Your musicians will get that information in the PDF you create and upload to the cloud folder.

For the OLD SCHOOL method, I would use the same plan as the ALTERNATE PLAN, but you print it out and distribute it.

NOTIFY MUSICIANS THAT THE MUSIC IS READY.

Once I have completed the service planning, I click on "send a message" in my online planning application, and it notifies my scheduled musicians that their music is ready. There is a link sent to them to the worship plan, so they can go there, download their music to their devices or printer, listen to the reference audio files, look at all the notes, and begin preparation for our rehearsal. As discussed earlier in the section, *Creating a Culture for Better Rehearsals*, they are expected to be familiar with the music before coming to rehearsal. They have every tool at their disposal to prepare well if I did my prep work as outlined here.

Since they receive the music more than a week ahead, there should be time to do that. I also try to prepare rehearsal tracks for the vocalists of each song with their parts being played or sung.

The ALTERNATE PLAN for notifying your musicians is to send out a message to your Facebook event page participants, email the group, or text the group. Give them a direct link to the cloud folder with all the necessary resources.

If you are going OLD SCHOOL, place the printed music, worship plan sheet, and digital media of audio files in their hands at least one week before their rehearsal. If needed, mail the package to them to ensure they have plenty of preparation time.

Once all that prep is done, it is time to move to the next stage:

REHEARSE!

Gather the band together and rehearse each piece. This should be done preferably on a day other than the day of the worship service. Work out the intricacies of each song. How do we introduce the song? What is the tempo? How do we play each part of the song? Just realize it is best not to play every verse, chorus, etc. the same way. How will we vary it? How can we best paint the words we are singing to connect with the congregation? How will we connect two or more songs in a worship flow? How do we end the song? I would allow at least an hour for this rehearsal. Your specific situation can cause that to vary greatly depending on the competence of your musicians and the difficulty and number of your arrangements. Always look for teachable moments for discipleship, as I described in the choir preparation section, including ways to help the band and singers connect with the lyrics of the songs they play.

Your vocalists would benefit from rehearsing their parts separately from the band at this time, then putting them together later in the rehearsal or in the worship run-through I will discuss next.

WORSHIP RUN-THROUGH

Meet with the band, vocal team, and tech team on the day of the worship service to go through every song in completion—just as if you were leading in the worship service, making any last-minute alterations that are needed. Ensure that all service cues are well understood (for instance, the drummer gives one bar count off immediately after the "amen" to begin the congregational song).

Now your preparation is done. You have sought God's guidance in planning; you have given your musicians every benefit to be excellent in their playing, and now you put it in God's hands as you lead in this time of worship.

> **What areas of band and vocal team preparation do you need to improve on?**

PREPARING THE MEDIA

In many churches, what goes on the screen is the responsibility of the worship leader and the pastor (the pastor primarily takes care of sermon slides). In many cases, volunteers may do much of the creation of the slides.

Think of the screen as a canvas upon which you create visuals used throughout the service to enhance the time of worship. Visuals are powerful communicators and should be carefully designed to engage the worshipper for the entire worship experience. Mediocre slides will speak a message you should not want.

USES FOR VIDEO

As you think through what will go on screen, here are eight uses for video in the church in no particular order:

ANNOUNCEMENTS

Spoken announcements can be a worship killer, especially if they fall in the middle of a service. Move most announcements to projected slides/videos early in the service or as people enter the sanctuary. Also, strongly utilize your church bulletin, newsletter, and social media. There are still a few announcements that need to be verbalized at appropriate times at the beginning and end of the service.

MISSION VIDEOS

Videos are a great way to highlight the mission causes and organizations your church supports; they can also provide informational support for upcoming mission offerings. Most mission organizations offer high-quality, free videos for your use. Check out the websites of the mission organizations your church supports for the video resources they provide. Including video summaries of your church's mission trips requires filming and editing, but it is rewarding to be able to tell the story of how God worked through your church's missions team in this way.

SHORT VIDEOS

There are many sources of great, short videos that can be used to enhance the morning sermon, introduce a song, or highlight a seasonal emphasis. You will also find many that make great calls to worship or meditations on Scripture. Short videos can be used as transitional elements in the flow of worship. If you have people with video creation talent in your church, you can produce your own. Check out a compilation of sources for short videos, or as they are often called, mini-movies, at WorshipMinistryGuidebook.com.

TESTIMONY VIDEOS

Videos of personal testimonies can help the church celebrate what God is doing in the members' lives. Sometimes handing a person a microphone on Sunday morning to speak can produce unwanted consequences, but filming the testimony and doing some great editing can produce a powerful, succinct testimonial video that can be shown in worship. These can be especially powerful before baptisms.

I have seen churches use video testimonies before baptism in a powerful way. Candidates previously have videos produced of them giving testimonies to their changed life in Christ. The videos are edited as needed to produce powerful testimonials. As each candidate walks into the waters of baptism, the footage shows the candidate's testimony, and then that person is baptized. This is a powerful way to relay the message of transformation and rebirth.

LYRIC DISPLAYS OF CONGREGATIONAL SONGS

This is probably the beginning place for a church to enter the video world. A note related to unified, intergenerational worship: Be careful not to make the mistake of many churches that only show the "contemporary" songs on screen and then sing the older songs from the hymnal. You may inadvertently create a division in your congregation by making the chasm even wider between different styles of music. Show all lyrics on screen or none at all. You may still announce/print/display hymn numbers so that people may choose to use the book or the screen. In my experience, very few people use the books after a few months, even though they first thought that was their preference.

GRAPHICS ON SCREEN FOR SERMON SUPPORT

Many pastors who use projected media only think of producing a PowerPoint presentation with an outline of the sermon, complete with flying bullet points and such. While this may be helpful to some in following the message, instead, think of ways to utilize images that capture the imagination to help drive home a point. The concept, "A picture is worth a thousand words," can be applied here. Short videos and movie clips can also be powerful. If you use movie clips, you must be aware of copyright issues and have the proper licenses.

ON-SCREEN IMAGES

At various times in the journey of the worship experience, consider using images to help guide the worshipper. If you have people with artistic skills in your church, they can create images that can be used in projection and other worship outlets such as displays, bulletins, and websites.

IMAGE MAGNIFICATION

If your worship center is large, you can use the video system to show close-ups of the pastor or others leading worship to aid communication.

I've touched on the primary ways that churches utilize on-screen media. There are other ways the church can enhance worship through projected images, but these are perhaps the most prevalent. Take time to imagine every moment of your service and intentionally plan what will be on screen.

Careful planning to utilize video with excellence is so important. Haphazardly throwing together media to use in worship can be more distracting than enhancing and, in fact, can hurt your services.

Worship planners can use many applications (software and web-based services) to compile and show the media during the service. Many churches use PowerPoint because they already have that software and may know how to use it. Unfortunately, PowerPoint is very limited in what it can do and is not designed to handle the needs of worship. There are many applications today that are designed specifically for worship.

Here are some thoughts about the weekly workflow as you prepare the video components of worship:

WEEKLY WORKFLOW

Get updates on special videos or other creative elements and supporting media needed. Weeks earlier, when the sermon information was determined for a given Sunday, the worship planners began to look for appropriate videos, if desired, to use in this service. It may have been professionally produced or created in-house. Information about these pieces should be entered into your online planning app, your spreadsheet, or Word doc to preserve the information for that service.

Look at the worship flow that you created for this service. Think through every piece of the service and determine what may enhance that part of the service with the use of the screen. Review the ideas in the listing I just discussed to prompt your thinking.

Determine the background you will use for the lyrics. You should determine if you will use a static background (image or solid color/gradient) or a moving (video) background. Will the background help reflect the words, or will it be merely a blank canvas upon which the words are displayed? Some churches utilize complex video backgrounds, while others prefer white words on a black background. The spectrum in between is large. Determine what is best for your setting.

I was leading a worship team on mission in Malaysia many years ago. We were leading in worship at a church, and I had brought my computer for the video screens. As was the custom in much of the United States at the time, I had moving videos to use behind the lyrics. Later, a college student I was working with commented on how distracting the movement was to her. I never really thought about the possibility of the background interfering with worship. She had a valid concern. Many churches have moved from complex video images to very simple ones, partly for this concern. Consider your setting and what communicates well and what distracts as you determine how to navigate backgrounds for lyrics.

Some parts of the service may or may not be enhanced with on-screen images. Some churches prefer something displayed all the time; others will have a blank screen part of the time. I would encourage you not to show your church logo in those times to fill space as I see many churches doing. Worship is not a time to build your brand, rather it is a time to build up Jesus.

Build your presentation. As you begin compiling the media for worship, open your presentation software and the worship flow for the service. Create a new playlist in the presentation software for that service as you reference your worship flow, and begin dropping in or creating all the components for the service from beginning to end. For instance, there may be running ad slides as people gather. Static image slides may help set the environment for prayer, the Lord's Supper, etc. You may want to display Bible passages on screen as they are read individually or publicly.

As you create each song, ensure that the lyrics and song map match what you intend to do in worship. This will help prevent wrong lyrics from being displayed on screen in the worship service. If you are singing with open hymnals and the screen, ensure the words on the screen match the ones in the hymnal.

For some presentation applications, you can also determine what is shown on the rear screen (a separate display) to help the worship leaders carry out their responsibilities. Be familiar with all the options and choose wisely to help the up-front leaders. Consider what is going to streaming or monitors in other areas of the church. I usually set up the stage display (rear screen) to show the current and next slide lyrics so the team always knows what is coming next. It produces much more confidence in their leadership.

Import sermon support graphics. Many pastors produce their own sermon support materials. If they are done in PowerPoint or Keynote, you can run them in their native applications or preferably import the slides into your worship presentation software for a more seamless and controllable experience. You export each slide as a PNG or JPEG and then import them into your presentation software. Be sure to export high-resolution files that match or exceed your display resolution.

Once all your media is compiled and ready to go, you should create a tech sheet to help guide the volunteers running the worship presentation. I create tech notes in my worship planning application that will print out on a personalized page for the technician, showing just the information they need.

By the way, don't forget to provide excellent training for your tech people. Help them be successful in their work by giving them the training to meet their needs.

> **What areas of media preparation do you need to improve on?**

PREPARING THE CONGREGATION FOR WORSHIP

If congregations gathered *prepared* for corporate worship each week, our times would be much more meaningful. As a worship leader, I realize that people sing best when they sing songs they know. I also know that personal worship is a prerequisite to corporate worship–private times of daily worship are important to corporate worship. **To help the congregation prepare for worship, I want to encourage personal worship during the week and give them tools to prepare for the congregational singing** – to help them get familiar with the congregational songs and the message. Many churches publish materials (online and/or hard copies) to help their congregations prepare (personally and as a family) for weekly worship. Here are some ideas that can prompt your thinking about how to best help your congregation:

CONTENT

What information do you want to get into the hands of your people to help them prepare? This is your opportunity to pour into the lives of your church members in helping prepare them for worship each week. Many components can be helpful in your distribution piece. Be careful not to make it too complex so people feel it will take too much time to engage. Worship is a vital element of the discipleship process. Include components such as these in your distribution piece:

SERMON PREPARATION

Give the Scripture passage and some information (perhaps a brief synopsis) to help people prepare for what will be presented in the sermon. Ask questions that will help the people engage with the sermon material.

PRAYER POINTS

Give specific prayer points that will help people prepare

their hearts for worship and lift up those planning and leading the times of worship. This is not your church's prayer list for those who are sick, grieving, etc. Instead, this is a list of prayer prompts to help people pray specifically for the worship service and the leaders. These are more kingdom-minded prayers. Here are some ideas: Pray for those who will lead in worship; pray that the Holy Spirit will move in our worship service, leading us to exalt Jesus Christ; pray that God will move us to share His love with our community; etc.

SONGS OF WORSHIP

You may include YouTube links to the songs, especially those that show the lyrics, so your congregation can worship with the songs throughout the week. Target the songs that may be lesser known. You might include a brief devotional related to the text of one of the songs as well. You could also include links to Amazon or iTunes for members to download songs they want to put on their media players. Spotify playlists are also helpful.

FOLLOW-UP FROM LAST WEEK

You may include questions and additional commentary for people to consider after last week's worship service to continue their engagement with God's Word for the day.

FAMILY WORSHIP CUES

Finds ways to help your families worship together at home. Create some family worship encounters that bring all generations together around the same truths. You can create material especially for family worship times related to the weekly emphasis.

DISTRIBUTION

Your prep piece can be distributed in several ways. One or more of these will serve your congregation best. A multi-faceted approach is most effective.

ONLINE CONTENT

Prepare a web page with weekly information readily accessible to various online platforms. This can be on your church's existing website or a special site built for this purpose.

SOCIAL MEDIA

Use Facebook, Instagram, Twitter, and other social media avenues to connect the content with your people during the week.

EMAIL

Consider weekly and/or daily emails with content for the week.

GROUP TEXTING

Send group texts with links to resources such as YouTube videos or the worship website.

DOWNLOADABLE/PRINTABLE PDF

Prepare a nice-looking one or two-page prep sheet for families to print out or view online.

PRINTED HANDOUT

Distribute the material at your corporate worship service for the coming week's content. (This method alone, of course, misses out on all who do not attend that week but assists those that do not have internet connectivity.)

Taking the time to produce this type of worship prep may bring you great dividends in creating worshipping disciples.

BEST PRACTICES

In my interim worship leader positions, I was doing a few things to help our congregation in this area:

- I created a congregational worship website that gave information about the sermon each week and provided a video with lyrics to every congregational song. The site also had links to many devotional sites for our congregation's use.
- I regularly posted to our church's Facebook page with links to the worship prep site and encouragement to prepare for worship.
- I embedded new song videos with lyrics on the church's Facebook page.
- I included prayer prompts for worship on the church's Facebook page.
- A weekly email was sent to the church members with a copy of the church bulletin, including the week's song list. There was encouragement for the congregation to go to the worship prep website (the URL was embedded) to better prepare for worship.
- The bulletin and on-screen announcements promoted the

webpage for worship prep.

Realize that each church is unique, and how you can best prepare your congregation should be tailored to meet your congregation's needs.

Having your pastor mention these resources regularly will create much interest in the congregation. At one church where I served, the pastor would mention how he, his wife, and their children would spend time throughout the week, singing the songs that were to be used in worship the coming Sunday. Just hearing him testify to how that helped their worship and their family worship times was an outstanding way to promote this among the congregation.

> **What steps can you take this week to begin helping your congregation prepare for gathered worship?**

PREPARING PERSONALLY FOR WORSHIP

By now, you have prepared all your musicians, congregation, and media teams for worship, but you must attend to one vital piece—yourself. This is so important. How do you, as a worship leader, personally prepare for the corporate worship service? This can make a powerful impact on your leadership. These are some ways I prepare for leading worship.

PREPARE SPIRITUALLY

Spend time with God throughout the week. Make worship a natural part of your life throughout the day.

- A great way to prepare specifically for the week's worship service is to spend time in private worship with the songs you will be leading. Meditate on the words. Let them impact your life. Read relevant Bible passages to the songs. Sing the songs to God as you personally offer your worship and praise. The more you worship with the songs during the week, the greater your leadership will be an overflow of your walk with God.

- Spend time in God's Word and prayer. Seek the heart of God for your life and ministry.

- When possible, get alone with God in your church sanctuary and pray for those who will be attending the service. Prayer-walk the room. As you walk the room, pray specifically for people by name and needs you are aware of. Play the piano or guitar while you sing the songs you will be leading Sunday in a time of personal worship.

The value of the spiritual part of personal preparation cannot be underestimated. For me, the time connecting with God in worship through these songs brings so much to my leadership in gathered worship. Praying specifically for God to move in the service while lifting up people by name is a powerful component of preparation. Additionally, at times I have invited others to join me in prayer walking the sanctuary on Sunday mornings before the service. Uniting hearts in this petition is a worthy exercise.

PREPARE YOURSELF FOR LEADERSHIP

TRANSITIONS & INTRODUCTIONS

In addition to the spiritual preparation, I take time to think about transitions between each element of worship. I especially focus on how I will introduce each song the congregation will sing. If the song is part of a set (two or more songs in succession), I also think about any verbal transitions needed during the musical segues/transitions that seamlessly link the songs together. It is almost always best to keep the comments concise and often best to let the lyrics speak for themselves (in other words, say no words of introduction). You may also be responsible for transitions between other elements of the worship service, so plan those as well. The next chapter will dive deeply into verbal transitions.

UTILIZING SCRIPTURE

I find quoting Scripture is one of the most powerful ways to introduce a song. I often use LifeWayWorship's Scripture suggestions that are found under the "additional information" tab on the song's page. TheBereanTest.com is another great resource. Commit to memory verses of praise. There will be times God will bring a verse to mind in worship as you lead. You can find a great resource for this at WorshipMinistryGuidebook.com.

WRITING OUT YOUR VERBAL TRANSITIONS

Once you have an idea of how you will introduce a song, write it out. Too often, worship leaders speak from the cuff, and they ramble without saying anything substantive. Writing it out helps you organize your thoughts and make them concise. You do not have to read what you wrote, but when you speak, you will be well-organized and clear in your communication.

COMPILING RESOURCES

Our church uses ProPresenter with the stage display feature. This is great for a confidence monitor, allowing you to see the current lyrics and the next slide coming up. I also prepare a one-page sheet for each song with lyrics as a backup, if needed. Additionally, I will prepare the notes I need for introducing songs. I also have a copy of the worship flow to refer to throughout the service. I generally use my iPad for all of this rather than printing multiple pages. (I typically load all of this plus lead sheets for every song on my iPad, using the app *forScore*. Each lead sheet has an attached mp3 for reference. I have everything I need for rehearsals and worship in that one place.)

> **As you come well-prepared, you will find that you have greater freedom in your worship and a greater ability to worship while leading.**

> **Are you preparing adequately to lead in worship each week? Which areas need the most work?**

FINAL THOUGHTS

Now that you have planned and prepared well, it is time to lead well. If you have done all the personal, spiritual, and musical preparation, as well as all the other pieces of preparation I have outlined, then commit your time to God and lead the church in worship. Keep the congregation's focus on God and not on the worship leaders. Set an environment, removing distractions that keep people from worshipping. The better you and your team prepare ahead, the more you will be able to truly worship as you lead. Celebrate the transformed lives that result in times of worship!

Give God the glory!

Leading Worship

The past chapters have set the foundations for worship and helped you with the planning and implementation of gathered worship. There are a few additional areas in leading worship that I am continually asked about—*speaking between songs and other elements of worship* and helping teams with *platform presence*; I will provide some guidance in those areas in this chapter. Also, I will discuss ways to successfully lead worship when you are called upon to lead a group of people from different churches coming together for a conference, rally, worship, or some other meeting. But first, I will share an article that has been published in eight languages and read by nearly 2 million people in 200 countries; its popularity has been due to the fact that it addresses a global problem—people aren't singing in worship in many churches. I have addressed this issue from many sides in this book already. This list of *Nine Reasons People Aren't Singing in Worship*[72] will be something of a review in most points as well as bringing up some additional points. There are many reasons not listed here, such as those related to the heart of the worshipper; I realize people with no relationship with Christ will have no reason to sing in worship. The reasons I have outlined here, instead, are targeted at worship leaders—things *we* may be doing to deter congregational singing. These are things we can counter once we recognize the problems.

NINE REASONS PEOPLE AREN'T SINGING IN WORSHIP AND WHAT TO DO ABOUT IT

Worship leaders worldwide are sadly changing their church's worship (often unintentionally) into a spectator event, and **people are not singing anymore**. Before discussing our present situation, let's look back into history. **Prior to the Reformation, worship was largely done for the people.** The music was performed by professional musicians and sung in an unfamiliar language (Latin). **The Reformation gave worship back to the people**, including congregational singing, which employed simple, attainable tunes with solid, scriptural lyrics in the language of the people. Worship once again became participatory.

The evolution of **the printed hymnal** brought with it an explosion of congregational singing and the church's love for singing increased.

With the advent of **new video technologies**, churches began to project the lyrics of their songs on a screen, and the number of songs at a church's disposal increased exponentially. At first, this advance in technology led to more powerful congregational singing, but soon, **a shift in worship leadership began to move the congregation back to pre-Reformation pew potatoes (spectators).**

What has occurred could be summed up as the re-professionalization of church music and the loss of a key goal of worship leading — enabling the people to sing their praises to God. Simply put, we are breeding a culture of spectators in our churches, changing what should be a participative worship environment to a concert event. **Worship is moving to its pre-Reformation mess.**

I SEE NINE REASONS PEOPLE AREN'T SINGING ANYMORE:

1. **They don't know the songs.**

    With the release of new songs weekly and the increased birthing of locally written songs, worship leaders are providing a steady diet of the latest, greatest worship songs. Indeed, we should be singing new songs, but too high a rate of new song inclusion in worship can kill the participation rate and turn the congregation into spectators. I see this all the time. I advocate doing no more than one new song in a worship service, and then repeating the song on and off for several weeks until it becomes known by the congregation. People worship best with songs they know, so we need to teach and reinforce the new expressions of worship.

2. **We are singing songs that are not suitable for congregational singing.**

    There are lots of great, new worship songs today, but in the vast pool of new songs, many are not suitable for congregational singing by virtue of their rhythms (too difficult for the average singer) or too wide of a range (consider the average singer—not the vocal superstar on stage). Some songs may not have lyrics suitable for a song to be used in gathered worship. I discussed earlier the process for selecting suitable songs for your congregation.

3. We are singing in keys too high for the average singer.

The people we are leading in worship generally have a limited range and do not have a high range. When we pitch songs in keys that are too high, the congregation will stop singing, tire out and eventually quit, becoming spectators. Remember that our responsibility is to enable the congregation to sing their praises, not to showcase our great platform voices by pitching songs in our power ranges. The best range of the melody is the C to C octave; however, many melodies extend beyond an octave. The extended basic range of the average singer is an octave and a fourth from A to D (with an occasional Eb).

4. The congregation can't hear the people around them singing.

If our music is too loud for people to hear each other singing, it is too loud. Conversely, if the music is too quiet, generally, the congregation will fail to sing out with power. Find the right balance — strong, but not overbearing. I have seen churches that pass out earplugs as you enter because the sound levels are so high. That certainly turns the room into more of a spectator event since you cannot hear the "corporate" part of worship—the people around you singing.

5. We have created worship services, which are spectator events, building a performance environment.

I strongly advocate setting a great environment for worship, including lighting, visuals, the inclusion of the arts, and much more. However, when our environments take things to a level that calls undue attention to those on stage or the cool technology and distracts from our worship of God, we have gone too far. Excellence — yes. Highly professional performance — no.

6. The congregation feels they are not expected to sing.

As worship leaders, we often get so involved in our professional production of worship that we fail to be authentic and invite the congregation into the journey of worship. We must facilitate the experience by singing familiar songs, introducing new songs appropriately, and singing in the proper congregational range. I had a friend ask me one day if I thought he was supposed to be singing in worship on a particular song the previous weekend. I asked him to explain what he meant. He said that their songs are mostly led by a male (who is their worship pastor), but on this particular song, one of the ladies in the group took the lead at the beginning. The lyrics were on screen, but none of the other vocalists were singing, and they were all looking at the lady who was leading the song. I commented that I think they probably intended for the congregation to sing, but they were suggesting to everyone with their actions that they were to just stand and listen to the lady sing. None of the other vocalists were singing. All of them were looking at the one singing. I always instruct vocal teams at times like that to continue singing and engaging the congregation (looking out at the congregation rather than the singer) without holding the mic to their mouths. The lady leading would be the only one heard, but people see that everyone is singing, and they would assume that it is expected for them to sing as well. As worship teams, we need to be sure we are not relaying contrary messages.

7. We fail to have a common body of hymnody.

With the availability of so many new songs, we often become haphazard in our worship planning, pulling songs from many sources without reinforcing the songs and helping the congregation take them on as a regular expression of their worship. In the old days, the hymnal was that repository. Today, we need to create song lists to use in planning our times of worship. On an additional note, with the vast number of songs available and no denominational clearing house to create a body of acceptable songs (the hymnal of previous days), today, every church may have a vastly different repertoire of songs. When there is little commonality, and a believer moves to another location and joins another church, they may not know the songs used at the new church, and they will be severely disabled in their worship. To offset this, churches should strive to have a large portion of their diet composed of songs more commonly sung in churches across their country. In countries where songs are reported through CCLI, one can consult those lists as discussed earlier in the book. Providing a diet of appropriately filtered songs from these lists will help ensure that churches have more of a common body of songs.

8. Worship leaders ad-lib too much.

Keep the melody clear and strong. The congregation is made up of people with limited ranges and limited musical ability. When we stray from the melody to ad-lib, people try to follow us and end up frustrated and quit singing. Some ad-lib is nice and can enhance worship (especially in instrumental sections of the song), but don't let it lead your people astray. There was a time I told worship leaders that ad-lib was probably fine when the congregation was singing a song that they know really well. Later, I was in a large East Asia country as part of a corporate worship experience with a couple of hundred people. They were singing, *How Great Is Our God*. The worship leader began to ad-lib on the chorus, and suddenly the congregation was no longer singing with might. People were searching to find the notes the leader was singing, trying to follow him in his ad-lib, but were unable to achieve it. The song just lost its power. Now, I recommend that the melody is always strongly heard by the congregation so that no other parts are overshadowing it.

9. Worship leaders are not connecting with the congregation.

We often get caught up in our world of amazing music production and lose sight of our purpose of helping the congregation to voice their worship. Let them know you expect them to sing. Quote the Bible to promote their expressions of worship. Stay alert to how well the congregation is tracking with you and alter course as needed. There are two aspects of connecting with the congregation that are necessary.

The first relates to our time on stage. In situations where lights are bright on stage and the house lights are dim or off, you may not be able to see the people you are leading. Using in-ear monitors often isolates you only to hear the band and vocals, but no congregational voices. It would be best if you remedied this by adjusting the lights so that you can clearly see the ones you are leading and by either removing one of your earbuds or adding congregational vocals (through a mic to pick up the congregation) in your in-ear mix so that you can hear the congregation sing.

The second area relates to off-stage life. As mentioned earlier, spending time doing life with the people in your congregation through fellowship, discipling relationships, mission project involvement, etc., will help you connect on a deeper level as you lead them in worship. Having a green room mentality of being the superstars on stage will only lead to creating a spectator mentality in the congregation.

> Once worship leaders regain the vision of enabling the congregation to be participants in the journey of corporate worship, I believe we can return worship to the people once again.

> Which of these nine areas needs work in your church? What are some steps you can take to remedy these problems?

SPEAKING BETWEEN SONGS AND OTHER ELEMENTS OF WORSHIP

There are times in the service when the worship leader can help the congregation in the journey of worship by speaking. It is vitally important that your verbal transitions are well thought out and planned ahead of time. Too often, worship leaders speak without preparation, and often the result is ineffective rambling that may hinder worship. Therefore, it is essential that you take time and script out what you will say at each juncture. Then, memorize the key points and rehearse what you will say overall. Make it conversational in tone. Writing out your speaking parts will help you organize your thoughts to make what you say valuable to the worship time.

I would encourage you to review several services from the past weeks and listen to the verbal transitions. Were they trite and overused statements, or were they substantive and well thought out so that they were valuable for the congregation's worship experience? Too often, we speak "off the cuff" only to provide fluff filler that does not help, but may hinder the worship.

You should not see yourself as a leader of songs that is checking off each song in the set. Instead, see yourself as a leader pastoring and guiding the 20-or-so-minute journey of worship. You will be conversationally pastoring the people through song, Scripture, and prayer.

> **Our goal is to honor God and help others bring their worship to the Lord.**

We should not strive to be slick. We need to show humanity. Think more like being family and less of creating a concert/big show venue feel.

Before you step on the platform, pray for the people you are about to lead. That will help you get your focus in the right place. *We are here to serve. Give us a heart for the people we are about to lead. Let us be mindful of the brokenness and difficulties people are walking through. Give us a sensitivity to your Spirit. Release your Spirit on this congregation right now.*

TYPES OF SPEAKING YOU CAN USE:

QUOTE SCRIPTURE

Using the Word of God in worship is powerful. Find ways to infuse your services with Scripture. Check out the verses of praise resource for lots of choice verses to commit to memory and use in worship (find the resource at WorshipMinistryGuidebook.com). Bible passages can inspire, instruct, admonish, convict, and so much more.

> EXAMPLE: "Psalm 30:4 says, 'Sing praise to the LORD, you His godly ones, and give thanks to His holy name.' Let's join our voices singing praise and giving thanks to our God this morning."

USE A PORTION OF THE SONG LYRICS

There might be a powerful portion of the song text that can be used to help focus people's worship.

> EXAMPLE: Using the song *His Mercy Is More* say, "What do you think about the fact that a Holy God can love sinners like you and me? That despite all our shortcomings, God loves us? As you sing this song, really shout out the gospel because while our sins are many, His mercy is more!"

LEAD IN A MINISTRY TIME

Consider having people thank God for their blessings or

confess their sins — based on what was just sung.

EXAMPLE: If you were singing *Blessed Be Your Name*, you could speak about the line that says, "every blessing you pour out, I'll turn back to praise," and encourage everyone to think of some blessing from this week that they can turn back to praise. "We just sang, 'Every blessing you pour out, we'll turn back to praise.' Have you taken the time to do that this week — to praise God for all He has done for you and the blessings He has poured out on you? Take a moment to offer Him praise right now where you are." As the music is playing underneath, give the congregation a moment to offer their praise. Then the music segues into a song such as *Your Name*, which provides the congregation with another way to voice their praise (and the song fulfills the textual link transition related to the name of God).

PRAY

Offer a prayer that ties in with what has just been sung or perhaps bridging to the next song idea.

EXAMPLE: *Way Maker* into *Goodness of God*. Say something like, "Father, you are our Way Maker, our Miracle Worker, our Promise Keeper, our everything. We come before you today, asking that you move in our midst and turn our lives around. Reach into our brokenness and bring hope and strength. Your mercy never fails us. You always hold us in your hands. Thank you for your faithfulness. ..."

SHARE SOME BACKGROUND OF THE SONG

Sometimes the story of the song can help engage people's minds and hearts in a great way as they connect with what they are singing.

EXAMPLE: *Victory in Jesus*: Say something like, "In 1939, a stroke rendered Eugene Bartlett partially paralyzed and unable to continue his popular gospel music career. He spent the last two years of his life bedridden. Amid such bleak circumstances, he wrote his final and most beloved song, *Victory in Jesus*, an optimistic number sung by millions in worship services and recorded by gospel's biggest names. As we sing this today, think that no matter what you are going through, as a child of God, you can declare VICTORY!"

THEME IDEA

There may be opportunities to weave in ideas from the sermon topic or other theme of the day to help connect the songs to the theme and engage the people's hearts and minds.

EXAMPLE: Using the theme, "Reaching the World for Christ," you can use the song *God So Loved* and say something like, "We are commanded to take the gospel to every corner of our world. We need to proclaim it to the weary and share it with the thirsty to come and find mercy at the cross because God so loved the world that He gave us His one and only Son to save us and whoever believes in Him will live forever."

WORSHIP TEACHING

You can interject sound bites in the service to help people understand what worship is, the focus of worship, acceptable postures of worship, etc. Scripture is powerful in proclaiming this as well.

EXAMPLE: Say something like, "Psalm 134:2 says, 'I will lift my hands in the sanctuary and bless the Lord.' Throughout the Bible, we find that worship is physically active and often involves lifting our hands in praise. As we sing this song, feel free to lift your hands in the sanctuary and bless the Lord for all He has done in our lives."

TEACH ABOUT AN ATTRIBUTE OF GOD

The church needs to understand and worship the various attributes of God. If a song you are using speaks to one of them, take a moment to help the congregation understand it. This is another area where you should use Scripture to illuminate truth.

EXAMPLE: Using the attribute of faithfulness, sing *Great Things* and say something like, "The Bible tells us that 'The faithful love of the Lord never ends! His mercies never cease. Great is His faithfulness; His mercies begin afresh each morning.' Our God is faithful. Amen? He may be safely relied upon. We can fully trust Him. Faithfulness is part of His divine character. No matter what you are going through today, just know that our God is faithful. He will not let you down or turn His back on you. Trust Him with everything." Segue directly into the song's second verse, "You've been faithful through every storm. …"

Welcome/admonition/instruction. See the section on opening/welcome below for details.

FIVE PRIMARY PLACES TO CONSIDER SPEAKING:

1. Opening/welcome

It is essential to build a bridge as quickly as possible with the congregation so they trust you. The first minute can set the atmosphere for the remainder of your leadership time by your posture and how you greet the congregation. You need to be your most authentic self. You are not a game show host. Be gentle. Speak to the congregation as you would to a group of friends to invite them into a time of worship.

> EXAMPLE: "Good morning. It's great to see everyone. Let's begin to find our seats and prepare our hearts to worship the Lord. Let's turn our conversations to the Lord as we begin to sing our prayers this morning (music begins). Let's stand together. ..."

I would strongly recommend you utilize Scripture in encouraging the people to join in worship — to help them place their focus on God. There are numerous verses of praise in the Bible that are very effective.

> EXAMPLE: "Good morning, friends. Welcome to church! As we begin to worship the Lord, let us look at the Scripture in Psalm 51:15: 'O Lord, open my lips, that my mouth may declare Your praise.' We have come together this morning to declare the praise of our God openly and boldly. Let's stand and open our mouths and let His praises sound forth. Let's declare His worth right now!"

During the welcome, we want to help people understand why we are doing what we are doing in worship (perhaps through a scriptural exhortation) and what is expected of them (stand, sing, praise God with your mouths, etc.).

If there is a particular emphasis or theme that day, you can set that up in the opening as well.

2. Before a song

You can use any of the ideas outlined in the *Types of Speaking* section as the intro of the song is being played. If the intro is strong, you might begin with quiet music moving to the strong intro at the completion of your speaking.

3. Within a song

In turnarounds to verses or extended interludes, you can help people by setting up the next stanza, quoting Scripture that is relevant to the song, or otherwise encouraging their worship and praise. It might be just a sentence that will help the congregation be more participative and connected in their worship of God.

4. At the end of a song

As you close out a song and the outro is playing, you can quote Scripture, pull a phrase from the song you just led that can help the congregation focus, or offer a prayer with closure in mind. Rather than ending there, you may spontaneously return to singing a portion of that song in a more unplugged manner (see the section on *planned spontaneity*).

5. Between songs

In most cases, you will want to connect songs seamlessly to flow smoothly, as discussed earlier in this book. However, you can craft instrumental music that connects the songs so that you can speak during this time. Here you can quote Scripture, pull a phrase from the previous song to help the congregation focus, or offer a prayer.

ADDITIONAL THOUGHTS

After you plan your worship flow, it will be essential to work through the plan to get a good feel for it. How will each element connect? What would be helpful to say, if anything? Once you decide where you should say something, write it out, memorize key points and rehearse it with the timing you will have. It should be rehearsed with the band so they can also be prepared.

If you are afraid of public speaking, immerse yourself in Scriptures that you can quote in worship. Commit many to memory. God will bring them to mind as you lead. As you continue to script and rehearse your comments, God will give you more confidence in leading His people in worship. Commit this to fervent prayer.

Realize, however, that too much talking will cause a break in continuity or progression. Some verbal transitions are helpful, but less is usually better. Short Scripture passages are best.

Do you need to plan out your verbal transitions with more intentionality?

PLATFORM PRESENCE

So often I see worship teams that seem stoic as they lead worship. Their facial features and body movements are not inviting, nor do they model what it means to be a worshipper. Too often, teams spend all their time dealing with musical issues, overlooking this critical piece of worship leadership.

With his permission, I have adapted much of this section from a podcast by Alex Enfiedjian[73]. Check out Alex's website: WorshipMinistryTraining.com for lots of great resources.

Jesus said the greatest commandment is to love the Lord your God with all your heart, soul, mind, and strength — that is your body. And in Romans 12:2, it says that we should offer our bodies as living sacrifices, which is our spiritual act of worship. So how can we use our bodies to worship God and lead others in worship? Did you know that your words only contribute to 7% of your communication? The rest is all body language, vocal inflection, facial expression, and posture. If our words are not accompanied by proper body language, our communication is weak. That's why it should matter to worship leaders (anyone on the stage leading—instrumentalists and vocalists). **We must care about our platform presence; we must use our bodies in a way that helps people connect with Jesus.**

> **How we hold ourselves on stage can either help or hinder people in worship.**

As worship leaders, we should not want our bodies and the way that we're standing or the way that our faces look to get in the way of people connecting with God. With that in mind,

here are eight simple tips that will hopefully improve your platform presence. There are seven do's and one don't.

1. **Be aware.** Be aware of what is going on with your body. Be aware of your posture, your hands, your facial expressions, and your weird quirks. Does your body reflect the joy of the Lord? One meaningful way we can improve is to smile as we lead. A smile can significantly impact the congregation. Additionally, it is a great help if you sing even if you're not a singer and even if your vocal part is not on mic at the time. Singing keeps you looking engaged in worship, which will be contagious to the congregation.

2. **Be confident.** If you look nervous, the congregation will be nervous with you, and that's a huge barrier. One of the best ways to build a look of confidence is to be well-prepared. Know your music thoroughly, and don't bury your head in the music stand. Memorize the music, if possible. As mentioned earlier in this book, if you are going to speak while leading, be prepared and rehearsed with what you will say.

3. **Be authentic.** People can generally tell when you are not being yourself. They can tell when you are not genuinely meaning what you are singing, when you are not truly worshipping, or when you are only going through the motions of worship. We need to be real. Shout for joy, cry, or move around. Be yourself. That is expressed differently from person to person. Use your body, but do it in a way that represents you and looks like you.

4. **Be an example.** Congregations reflect their leaders. If we

are bored or unengaged on the stage, the congregation will probably be bored and unengaged. Why should we expect that they're going to be crying out and lifting up their hands and worshipping the Lord with passion if we're not doing it? They're just reflecting what they're seeing us do. **We help the congregation engage passionately when we show them how.** Show them how to be an example. We need to spur them on with our bodies.

5. **Be obedient to the Scriptures.** We seem to have the "sing to the Lord" command down, but that is often the extent of our obedience. How about the commands to raise and clap our hands, dance and shout for joy, and shout aloud? As you follow the Scriptures in your actions, you will be teaching the congregation as well, and leading by example.

6. **Be engaged.** Open your eyes, engage with the congregation, look out at the room, smile and be present. Be in the moment — enjoy the worship going up to our good Father. Seeing them worship can help you worship.

7. **Be in control.** Use your body to lead the congregation. Use your body to help the congregation know when to begin singing. Turn your attention to whoever might be speaking, reading Scripture, etc., to help the room focus on what is important. Be careful not to draw attention to yourself.

8. **Don't be a distraction.** Worship leading is the art of removing distractions. Don't wear inappropriate clothing that will be a distraction. Make sure your movements are appropriate to your context.

> **Use your body as a tool to lead people rather than as a distraction to dissuade people.**

For further study, check out an instructional video on platform presence at WorshipMinistryGuidebook.com

> **Remember that you have been called to use your body as a tool to worship God and as a tool to lead your church in worship.**

> **Review a video of your worship team leading a recent service. What does your team need to work on to communicate better with their platform presence? What do you need to work on personally?**

REMOVING BARRIERS TO CONNECTING WITH THE CONGREGATION

Recently, I attended a worship service in which physical barriers were a hindrance to leadership. In the service, an excellent soloist sang a moving song that had tremendous potential to communicate a powerful testimony. The soloist stood in the choir loft, behind a music stand, behind a grand piano, behind a choir railing, behind pulpit furniture (chairs, enormous pulpit, etc.), and read from her music as she sang. There was little to no emotional connection with the congregation. A radical transformation would occur if the soloist were to memorize her music, stand on the stage to the side of the pulpit with no barriers between her and the congregation, and sing the song while connecting powerfully with the congregation. The same song and soloist would have made a greater impact in that service. **Worship leaders should strive to remove the physical barriers that hinder their role.**

Similarly, the choir needs to strive for barrier removal. One of the greatest barriers a choir has is the folder. Once the choir memorizes the music and begins to worship the Lord as they sing, the worship becomes contagious to the congregation. They begin to draw the congregation into worship, rather than communicating that they should sit and listen to the great performance by the choir.

I mentioned earlier the importance of the choir memorizing their music. Dave Williamson, in his book, *God's Singers*, exhorts **the benefits of a choir memorizing their music:**

- The choir sings better, and more freely.
- The picket fence (folder barrier) is removed, allowing the congregation to feel closer to the choir as its worship leader.
- The choir's hands are freed up to be used in biblical postures of worship.
- The choir's faces are drawn upward, every countenance now visible.
- The choir senses one another's presence and is much more able to join hearts as well as voices in the act of leading worship.
- The choir feels closer to the congregation, and is able to more effectively lead them in worship.
- Most importantly, the choir is free to concentrate its whole being on the act of worshipping God, which is the first

and most necessary step in the process of leading others to worship Him.[74]

The same comments I have made here about the choir and soloists also apply to vocal teams. Look for ways to remove the barriers between the singers and the congregation.

> Evaluate your singing worship leaders. Are they creating a spectator environment in your church, or are they helping the people really worship? Are there physical barriers impeding their leadership? What can you do to transform your singers in this way?

PLANNING A WORSHIP EVENT FOR PEOPLE FROM DIFFERENT CHURCHES AND WORSHIP STYLES

I often lead worship in events that have participants from many churches. These churches represent various worship styles and worship music repertoires. Some sing only from an open hymnal and utilize only a few, if any, modern worship songs. Some sing only the most current music. Some churches worship with only an organ or a piano, while others utilize a worship band. Some have choirs; others use vocal teams. Some churches are anywhere in between on this spectrum.

Planning worship for these events can be challenging. For people to be participative in worship, we need to use songs they know, yet if you had a list of every song each person attending the event knows, you may find that there are few commonly-held songs. In addition, I find it important to utilize a wide variety of songs to connect with each person in their heart language. So how do we best create a worship environment where our people can participate and worship?

1. **I pray for God's guidance in selecting the music and planning the worship times.**

2. **I select a variety of songs** (when written, style, etc.) to incorporate in the times of worship.

3. **I draw from the most widely known songs of those periods and styles.** Looking at CCLI lists helps me to select songs that are more commonly known by congregations.

4. **I make sure we sing all the songs in keys accessible by the vast majority of the people.** I have written extensively on this topic, but the bottom line is that the melody should ideally fall between C and C, with wider-range songs being in the A to D with an occasional Eb range. Singing outside of this range leads to a lack of participation.

5. **When possible, I try to incorporate a variety in worship leadership.** Consider utilizing a choir, an orchestra, a vocal team, a rhythm section/band, a horn section, etc.

6. **I prepare a worship aid that has every song we will sing** with a YouTube video embedded, including lyrics to help people learn the music. If possible, I send this to each participant ahead of time and ask them to begin learning songs

they do not know during their personal times of worship so they have more meaningful times of corporate worship when we gather for the event. This has been a massive help for events in the past and has brought so much affirmation from participants.

7. **I pray that God will engage the congregation in worship,** laying aside personal preferences and biases related to the songs we are using and just lift up Jesus.

A few years ago, I was invited to lead the musical portions of worship for a large conference. In the past, the meeting had always been led in a very traditional-styled approach using traditional hymns and accompaniment. The event organizers wanted me to instead lead with a band and vocal team incorporating modern worship styles. I admit I was really concerned about how involved the congregation would be. I planned all the times of worship and prepared a webpage with all the songs as embedded YouTube videos and some instructions. All the participants were urged to prepare ahead. To my amazement, the congregation was one of the most participative congregations I have ever led. The hundreds of voices rang out strongly with passion. I believe our great success in this was due to following the guidelines I listed above. Pray, prepare yourself, and help participants prepare.

Perhaps one of the most outstanding examples of preparing the people ahead of time was during the years of the Promise Keepers' rallies that would fill ball stadiums around the country with men worshipping God. After people registered for the event, they received a cassette (yes, you read that correctly) with all the songs used in worship. Men would listen to the music over and over for weeks before going to the rally. Once there, the singing was deafening as the men passionately proclaimed their worship of God. That would not have happened without the preparation.

Of course, there are many times that preparing the congregation ahead by sharing resources is not possible. In those cases, you can strive to accomplish all the points above except that one. Leading such a gathering is indeed a great joy.

Can you think of an example of this type of event that you may have the opportunity to lead? It might be a meeting of area churches, a men's or women's conference, or a missions rally. How would you approach such an opportunity in planning and implementation?

Evaluating Worship

A crucial part of improvement is continually evaluating anything you seek to improve. This holds true in worship leadership. As you make changes and seek to improve yourself as a worship leader and your church's worship ministry, you must regularly evaluate your progress.

To evaluate your leadership and your ministry, you must have some goals or standards that you are seeking to reach.

One place to start is for your worship team to discuss what they feel is a God-sized vision for your worship ministry. Here are some examples:

- A church where people are eager to come and meet God every week.
- Worship teams who are totally committed to the task to which God has called them and who seek to improve and grow in their relationship with God and musicianship.
- All generations truly worshipping together and offering a sacrifice of praise.

These are worthy goals.

What do you feel God would
have your team aspire to?

In addition to working with your worship team to determine some goals for the ministry, I encourage you to go back through this book and **set some tangible goals for your life and ministry.** A ministry goal could be one of the ones from the list above. Perhaps an individual goal would be for you to be more comfortable speaking and transitioning between elements of worship or to be better at balancing spirit and truth in leading worship.

Whatever you sense God is leading you to strive for, you should **set some tangible steps to reach those goals.** Set action steps and deadlines to keep you working at it. For instance, you may feel you need to have verses of praise memorized that you can easily interject into times of worship. You set an action step of memorizing one verse each week while reviewing previous weeks throughout the first six months. In six months, you have 26 verses committed to memory. Perhaps you set a goal of being better at leading your church in planned spontaneity moments. Your action steps could involve spending a few hours each week creating and rehearsing these types of transitions for a month, then introducing one of these moments into gathered worship every three weeks. These steps would help your worship team adapt to these moments with a spontaneous feel.

This should be a continual process of setting goals for improvement, striving for those goals, and evaluating your progress. When you feel you have reached the goal, seek God for the next steps in improvement. Highlight places in this book where you feel God is speaking to you about areas that need addressing. Continually review the material and evaluate how you and your church are doing in these areas. The evaluation checklist coming up next will be a great way to point out areas of need and concern.

The following assessment engages much of what I have discussed in this book to help you better see the connection of the material to your worship services each week. For an excellent evaluation covering many non-musical areas of worship, from when a person arrives on campus until departure, check out a resource on WorshipMinistryGuidebook.com.

WORSHIP EVALUATION CHECKLIST

When was the last time you did an honest evaluation of your worship service? I'm not talking about just sitting around on Monday morning asking, "How did it go Sunday?" While that kind of evaluative interchange can be helpful, a much more intensive evaluation will be better at helping us give our best to God in worship.

I suggest that you video your services and then sit down with your key leaders, the entire worship team, choir, or others, and give an honest evaluation of the service. The video will help significantly with some of the areas of the assessment, while other areas would be best evaluated only in the live service. I encourage you to personally review these questions each Monday as you reflect on Sunday. You may find it helpful to review them in light of the worship service you have planned in a couple of weeks as well!

I have compiled a number of questions below to aid you in

the evaluation:

VISUAL

- Were facial expressions of the vocal team/band/choir appropriate for worship?
- Was the team's platform presence appropriate for worship?
- Was each member physically engaged in a way to invite congregational participation?
- Was the team an excellent example of participative worshippers?
- Was anyone's movements distracting or seeming to draw attention to themselves?
- Was the team's attire modest and appropriate? Did it reflect your congregation?
- Was the stage set up in a functional way with clear sightlines?
- Were the aesthetics of the stage conducive to worship?
- Was accent lighting and other lighting conducive to worship without creating a concert venue feel?
- Were the words/images on the screen clear to all seats?
- Was the overall worship environment conducive to participative worship, or did it seem more like people were attending a show?

MUSICAL

- Did all members of the team seem to know the songs well?
- Were the songs played at the correct tempo?
- Were vocals sung on key?
- Were instruments played in tune?
- Were the worship leader's cues noticeable and easy to follow?

- Were harmonies accurate and appropriate?
- Were songs done in appropriate keys for congregational singing?
- Was anyone distracting by being too flashy in their playing/singing or unprepared and not excellent in their presentation?

TECHNICAL

- How was the overall house mix?
- Was the decibel level appropriate?
- Could the congregation hear those around them singing well (i.e. the platform music was not drowning out the congregational singing)?
- Were vocals heard clearly?
- Was the melody always predominant?
- Were instruments blended well?
- If not using in-ear monitors, were the monitor mixes suitable?
- Did the projected images enhance or hinder worship?
- Did lyric slides change early enough for the congregation to be confident of the next line?

ENGAGEMENT

- Do you feel like the congregation was connecting with God in worship?
- Does the worship service engage the people actively in ways other than singing (such as praying in small groups, reading Bible passages aloud, sharing with others how God is at work, praying at the altar, bringing offerings to the front,

moving for Lord's Supper, etc.)?

- What physical gestures, movements, and postures were the congregation invited to participate in (such as raising hands, clapping, uplifted head, bowed head, clapping, swaying, processionals/recessionals, kneeling, standing, prostration, arms open, raising hands, and upturned palms)?
- Were all generations seemingly engaged in worship?
- Are you intentionally planning worship to be unified?
- Were steps taken to prepare the congregation for gathered worship by providing resources during the week to guide them in their preparation?
- Did the congregation always know they were expected to sing on the congregational songs (For example, were all the worship team members engaged even when only one vocalist was singing on mic)?
- Did the worship team always have a visual and aural awareness of the congregation (i.e. lighting and audio did not negate the congregation from their constant awareness)?

FLOW OF WORSHIP

- Was the opening/welcome well thought out and presented to help put people at ease and invite them in to worship?
- How was the overall flow of worship?
- Were transitions between elements of worship done well?
- Did transitions show variety (quote Scripture, use song lyric excerpt, lead in a ministry time, pray, worship teaching, share the background of the song, teach about an attribute of God, or connect with a theme)?
- Were the verbal transitions substantive and meaningful?
- Were the musical transitions between songs well executed

and helpful in providing a seamless flow?

- Was text link or thematic link involved in any of the song transitions to better connect heart and mind?
- Were there any interruptions to a smooth flow and direction in worship?
- Were announcements kept to a minimum and only included at the very beginning or end of worship?

SPONTANEITY

- Were there times of planned spontaneity? If so, how well were they executed? How well did they engage the congregation effectively?
- Were there times in the worship service that you went "off script" to follow the leading of the Spirit? How well did the musicians and tech team follow? How effective did it seem with the congregation? Do you need to rehearse how to handle these times in the future with your team?

EFFECTIVENESS AND DISCIPLESHIP

- How effectively do you think the team led the congregation into God's presence?
- Suppose this service is the only discipleship a church member receives this week. How well did you plan and implement the prayers, Scripture readings, songs, and transitions to intentionally disciple the congregation?

SONGS

- Are you utilizing a song list in your worship planning?
- Did all the songs you used pass through the biblical and

musical filters discussed in this book?

- Are the songs used in worship showing some variety (hymns, modern hymns, classics, modern worship songs, etc.)?
- Did you limit new songs in worship to no more than one?
- Were new songs introduced in the manner outlined in the book?
- Have new songs been reinforced by repeating them three weeks in a row?
- Did you feel any of the songs you did this week were too long or repetitive for the congregation (the congregation seemed less engaged as the song continued on)?

PRESENTATION

- Were songs played the same way for every verse, chorus, and bridge, or was there variety throughout the song creating various textures and feels?
- If presentational/representational music was used, did the presenting group come across as worship leaders or a performance group?

CHOIR

- If a choir was utilized, was that choir perceived as a worship-leading choir?
- Did each member look physically engaged in congregational and presentational songs?
- Did each member have pleasant expressions?
- Do you feel the choir was a catalyst for participative worship?

CREATIVE ELEMENTS

- How effective were the service's creative elements of worship, such as drama, images, readings, paintings, interpretive movement, and video?
- Were the elements prepared and presented with excellence?
- Did they help engage the hearts and minds of the worshippers?
- Did using these creative elements point people to God rather than attract attention to the person presenting?

PRAYER

- Were prayer times a substantive and effective modeling of prayer to help disciple your congregation?
- Were spontaneous prayers in the service substantive or full of overused phrases?
- Were people encouraged to take a posture of prayer, such as kneeling, hands uplifted, or lifted eyes?
- Were people encouraged to be more participative in prayer times by praying aloud, praying with others, or silently praying guided prayers?

CONCERNS

- Are prayer and personal worship stressed with your teams?
- Were you and your teams spending time in prayer for the worship service and the participants and leaders throughout the week?
- What specific things are hindering effective leading?
- What (if any) have been recent technical difficulties that need to be addressed?

- What (if any) musical issues (singing off key, performance issues, instruments too loud, and other issues) need to be addressed?
- Are there relational issues or difficulties among the team members which need to be addressed?
- Are there spiritual issues in need of being dealt with in any of your team members?
- Are there commitment problems that need to be dealt with?
- Was your pastor actively engaged throughout the worship service?

ADDITIONAL THOUGHTS

These questions are merely suggestions to help structure your times of evaluation. Why not make plans now to evaluate an upcoming service? What other questions do you think are important to the process?

MORE FOOD FOR REFLECTION AND EVALUATION

A LETTER FROM A CONCERNED WORSHIPPER AND MY RESPONSE

While we are discussing the evaluation of our times of corporate worship, it might be helpful to pull together themes from this material in a different way. I often receive emails from blog readers around our country commenting on worship practices (both positive and negative) in their churches. I received the following email as I was completing the book manuscript, and it seemed timely in view of my heightened awareness of the disconnect between many worship "productions" and true corporate worship. This letter echoes the sentiments of many comments I receive (*from both young and old*). In a sense, the worshippers are evaluating worship services they attend. **Hearing their perspective is vital to our overall evaluation of the services we lead.** I believe it also provides a good recap of several matters discussed in the book's earlier chapters.

> **REMEMBER THIS:**
> Worship practices grow from the underlying basic understanding of what worship is and the role of the worship leader. When those foundations are incorrect, the resulting worship practices are likewise unhealthy.

This book has established those foundations, and in this response, you can see how some of those play out in church ministry.

EMAIL

This is the email I received (author's name withheld):

For the last four weeks, my wife and I have been attending a church that is new to us. We are prayerfully looking for a church in which to invest our lives. After four weeks of attendance, I am thinking we will be looking for another church. Here is what we are experiencing:

- *Haze machines*
- *Programmable lights that blind the audience when they shift from shining really cool patterns on the ground to blasting light up into the ceiling.*

- *Singing songs we can't follow, most of which we've never heard. The melody is unmemorable. Very few in the audience seem to know the songs either; indeed as we looked around during one of the songs, we did not see one person singing—not one.*
- *Some of the songs are so high that I cannot sing them. I wish the leaders would consider the average singer!*
- *We arrived just as the music started one week and had to stand in the back for a while to let our eyes adjust to the darkness before looking for a seat. You could hardly see the people in the congregation.*
- *Today I came so close to walking out during the second song because it was creating pain in my ears. Driving home, my wife indicated that the excessive loudness was starting to cause some serious anxiety. Having earplugs available in the lobby is a sure sign there might be a problem.*
- *This Sunday, they must have failed to do a sound check because it took them well into the second verse of the first song before they had the vocals even close to being mixed. You literally couldn't hear the backup singer at all, and the lead vocal was indistinguishable because the instruments were so loud.*

We know lots of people our age who feel the same way as do their children. I know several adults in their early 20s who only go to this church for the great sermons; they cringe at the music.

Why does just about every praise and worship song go up an octave and double in volume halfway through, then die back down at the end?

Why do so many of the worship leaders wear ball caps when practically no one in the congregation is doing so?

We had a friend attend with us one week that is a professional audio tech for major concert artists. His biggest takeaway, besides the fact that the mix was not good, was that even if people in the congregation were singing, (which very few were), there was no way you could hear them. That's part of corporate worship–singing with the saints around you, ushering in the presence of the Holy Spirit, letting your heart be moved to tears, being broken.

So now we're trying to figure out what to do–keep going to this church and arrive just as the sermon begins because their preliminary "worship experience" does absolutely nothing towards bringing us closer to the throne, or possibly trying another church and listen to this church's sermon podcast later in the week.

It's interesting that one of the consistent comments about the recent revival at Asbury is that surprisingly there were no fog machines, no fancy lights, no thumping bass and crashing cymbals, and no worship leaders with baseball caps on backward and big holes in their jeans. It was just simple worship . . . and the Holy Spirit showed up big time. They weren't "feeling" the music; they were experiencing the Divine.

THE TAKEAWAYS

I believe in excellence in every way in worship. We should utilize technologies to assist our ministries where they can help us. Backing tracks (STEMS), in-ear monitors, lighting, and awesome audio and video equipment can all assist us in leading our congregations in worship that is life-changing. However, we can also abuse these tools in a way that distracts from helping our people worship.

As worship leaders/planners, we need to identify and elim-inate as many distractions as possible to create an environment that helps people connect with God. Further, we, as worship leaders, must see ourselves as prompters or guides, who help the people to participate in offering their worship and praise. We should never envision ourselves as performers and the congregation as an audience. Instead, we need to help the people experience God without calling attention to ourselves.

Let's unpack that a bit as I respond to that email.

LIGHTS AND FOG

Just as awe-inspiring architecture in old church buildings can set an excellent environment for worshipping God, lighting, and the use of fog, can help create a sacred space, when used with care and moderation, especially in architecturally plain worship spaces. **We need to determine what is helpful in establishing an environment in which people can worship and what causes distractions** (such as calling attention to the cool lighting effects or even annoying light in the eyes). As worship leaders, we need to be wise in utilizing these gifts in a way that enhances worship, rather than distracting from it.

I love how David Manner said it in a social media post:

> *We must be careful our worship service innovations don't cause us to focus more on the creative than the Creator.*

SONGS

As mentioned earlier, in my extensive surveys and work with churches, I find that two of the most significant ways worship leaders turn their congregations into spectators are through singing songs people do not know and singing in keys that the average singer cannot attain. For people to be participative in worship, they must sing songs they know. While new songs are vital to worship and biblically mandated, worship leaders have to be wise in introducing and reinforcing new songs through repetition. Also, if we want people to move from spectators to the biblical model of physical involvement in worship, we must sing songs in keys that are attainable to the average singer.

As I pointed out earlier, **a worship leader's calling is to help the people sing with all their being, even at the sacrifice of some things we, as musicians, would prefer. Worship is not about impressing the congregation with our extraordinary vocal skills; instead, our task as worship leaders is to enable others to worship.**

As the writer stated in the email, many songs today have octave jumps that provide a great sense of declaration and power. However, when that occurs, the average singer is often left behind, unable to follow the platform singers. As a result, the average singer gives up on participating and moves into a spectator mode. **If a song has a range beyond the ability of the average singer, we should either adapt the song or negate using it in worship.** There are plenty of great songs that can be substituted for that one.

The writer also mentioned melodies that are not memorable. **Worship leaders should choose excellent songs with melodies that live on** once the person leaves the time of corporate worship. Unfortunately, we often push songs on the congregation that cannot be remembered a few minutes after completing the song. We should strive to provide a diet of the best lyrics and melodies for our people.

As worship leaders, not Christian music artists, we must do all we can to help our people sing the songs with all their might.

LEVEL OF SOUND AND ROOM LIGHTING

I hear this complaint often: "The music is too loud in worship. It physically hurts the ears." There are times that we want to raise the roof with a great sound of voices and instruments. There are times we want to let a cappella voices fill the space. There are levels everywhere in between that we want to utilize to express our worship. However, when the band and singers get too loud, we once again encourage a performance environment rather than participatory worship. Music that is too loud also negates the biblical imperative that worship should be vertical (congregation to God) and horizontal (congregant to congregant) in nature:

> *Speak to one another with psalms, hymns, and spiritual songs. Sing and make music in your heart to the Lord, always giving thanks to God the Father for everything, in the name of our Lord Jesus Christ.* (Ephesians 5:19–20).

This passage brings up an important point discussed in the first chapter: Gathered worship has a horizontal and a vertical element. Not only is our worship directed to God as we offer Him our praise and worship, giving thanks for all He has done, but it also requires us to "speak to one another" in declaring His worth, testifying of His goodness, and sharing other tributes of God.

In churches like the one described in this letter, lights are so dim in the congregation that you are unaware of those throughout the room, and the music is so loud you cannot hear yourself sing, let alone others around you. This leads to a genuine sense that the "audience" has come to a performance. Therefore, they stand and do not participate, as the writer shared in his observation. When you cannot see nor hear your fellow worshippers, the existence of the corporate body journeying together in this act of worship is denied.

WORSHIP LEADER ATTIRE

This is an area I really did not want to mention. Still, when a puzzled 20-some-year-old asked me why worship leaders wear those ball caps on the platform, I decided it is not an over-40 issue, but **worship leader attire may be a distraction to many in the congregation.** I believe worship leaders should look like the congregation. **We should not be setting ourselves apart as an elite subculture that looks and dresses differently from our church.** We should not be calling attention to ourselves. You probably have seen all the social media memes making fun of the caps, toboggans, skinny jeans, Chuck Taylors, and various other apparel. This is a common observation among our congregations. I merely ask the question, "Is there a reason why the worship team should appear as different from the others in the congregation?" What is our heart's motivation in this? I don't personally find this too distracting, but from the comments I get from so many of *all ages*, there is an issue here. I think this should gain some weighty introspection of worship leaders.

LANDING THIS PLANE

I now ask the question: Are people today looking for a more authentic, biblical worship experience, void of the trappings of a high-production environment with lights, fog, loud music, worship leader subcultures, and more?

I think the writer of this letter said it well:

Interestingly, one of the consistent comments about the recent revival at Asbury is that surprisingly there were no fog machines, no fancy lights, no thumping bass and crashing cymbals, and no worship leaders with baseball caps on backward and big holes in their jeans. It was just simple worship . . . and the Holy Spirit showed up big time. **They weren't "feeling" the music; they were experiencing the Divine.**

Have we become so programmed that there is no room left for the Spirit to move? Have we become so performance-driven that our people are no longer involved in participative, transformational worship?

I encourage you to ask God to search your heart, rather than perhaps feeling insulted or defensive. Is the worship ministry you lead truly engaging the people in biblical, participative worship that is changing lives?

Do you and your worship ministry need to get back to the heart of worship?

Perhaps go "old school" one week soon, and get rid of the fog machines, programmed lights, and similar things, and see if you can just focus on leading people into a meeting with the God of this universe.

Final Words

There has been quite a lot of content presented in this book. I pray that you will take this material and seek God's heart as to ways He would lead you to improve as a worship leader and how He would direct change in worship at the church He has entrusted you to lead. Worship leading is a great privilege and joy, but it is also a great responsibility. For those called to a task, God will give us all we need to fulfill our calling if we seek Him and strive to get the training and knowledge we need to serve Him better. I applaud you for taking the time to read this book. I hope you will go back over sections regularly and ask, "How can I improve in this area?" Learning and improving are life-long processes. Every time I teach this material, I am convicted of how I fall short or take shortcuts. I need to review this material regularly and ensure that I serve my congregation well, making disciples of them, helping them participate in worship, and then witnessing transformation.

I usually close my in-person training with an illustration that I will share here:

In my mission work over the years, I have served several times in a closed country that has a monarch I will refer to as "the king." The story I am about to tell is fabricated, and I will use the fictional country of Kamaria instead of the country's real name.

FIRST VERSION

Our mission team was in Kamaria to encourage and equip the church. We were there for several days leading conferences and worship times. The king of Kamaria was always looking for ways to improve relations with the U.S.A. He heard that there were some visitors from the U.S. in his country, and he had one of his people reach out to me and invite me over for dinner—just me and the king. I could hardly believe I had received such an invitation! Dinner with the king! I understood he lived in a palace that far exceeded the size and splendor of Buckingham Palace. I had been told it was a fantastic place to behold. I asked my host family if I could borrow their car and go to the palace for dinner. They graciously agreed.

I drove to the palace, was allowed in by their security personnel, and drove to the entrance of the massive estate. I was greeted by the royal valet, who took my car to park in the garage. He directed me to the front entrance where the butler welcomed me. He was an amiable middle-aged man who ushered me in, took my jacket, and then had me sit in a parlor to wait for the meal. He sat with me and began to talk to me about the king. The king is a wonderful person with great compassion for Kamaria's citizens. He is just and fair in his dealing with people and is wonderful to spend time with. The butler attempted to put me at ease, so I would not be tense in our time of fellowship over the meal. I learned more about the fantastic ways the king loves his people and strives to make Kamaria the best country on earth. By the time he ushered me into the royal dining room, I was ready to be in the king's presence. I knew areas of discussion that would engage the king if there was a lull. I knew ways to praise him for all the great things he had done for the citizens of Kamaria. I felt I had a familiarity with him before even entering the room.

Our dinner was excellent. The food was world-class, and the conversation flowed throughout. I felt a bond with the king as the dinner was coming to a close. After the dinner, the king warmly said goodbye to me, and the butler entered to usher me out. He gave me my jacket, and we exchanged some additional words; then he directed me to my car waiting for me at the bottom of the stairs. I drove home, relishing my time with the king. It was indeed a great night I would cherish forever.

SECOND VERSION

I was in Kamaria with a missions team when I received the invitation to have dinner with the king. I borrowed my host's car, proceeded through palace security, passed my car along to the valet, and then climbed the steps to the front door. The butler greeted me at the door, took my jacket, and ushered me into the parlor to wait for dinner. The butler sat with me and began to engage me in conversation. Since I love international food, we talked about food in Kamaria, and I learned about his favorites and places in the city he particularly likes. We talked about special spices they use in Kamaria. I spoke with him about my favorite foods in the U.S. as well as favorites in several other countries. We laughed about some of the foods we had encountered in foreign lands and confessed we had eaten some pretty disgusting items. He mentioned that his son, a senior in high school, is interested in going to college in the U.S. He asked me about some specific colleges, and I relayed information about colleges I was aware of. We talked about potential majors and what it is like in different regions of the U.S. The butler asked me questions about my family, and I received information about his wife and three children. I got some insights into what it is like to serve the royal family. We talked for a couple of hours, then I took my jacket, and he ushered me to the door where my car was waiting at the bottom of the stairs. I entered my car and started my drive home. About halfway home, I realized, "I never saw the king!" I had gone to the palace to meet the king and have dinner with him, yet I never saw him!

Being a worship leader is very much like being a butler. We usher people into the presence of God by planning, rehearsing, and leading in a time of worship that was carefully prepared and bathed in prayer. Unfortunately, studies show that the vast numbers of people who come to gathered worship indicate that they never feel they encounter God in worship. Too often, we may be like the butler in the second illustration. We engage the people in great conversations, entertaining moments, and memorable times, but we never properly prepare them and usher them into the King's presence. Too often, worship is about slick songs and amazing presentations, rather than simply meeting God. God, forgive us when we make worship about ourselves rather than about You.

Our responsibility as butlers is tremendous. Will we strive to be like the butler in the first illustration who helps prepare people to meet with God and provides help along the way in expressing their love, worship, and praise to their Creator?

I hope this book has helped you think through and implement ways to do just that.

Worship leaders, you should:

- Prayerfully select the right songs and other components of worship
- Plan your approach to transition and flow as you create the service
- Resource your teams
- Rehearse your teams
- Prepare your congregation
- Prepare yourself
- Lead
- Evaluate and improve

I hope that this book has been and will continue to be a help to your ministry. It has been a pleasure journeying with you through these pages!

I pray that you will rise to the calling God has placed on your life and lead people weekly into the transformational presence of God. To God be the glory!

> **Stop right now and ask God to guide you in this journey of worship leadership. Pray that He will impress upon you the ways He wants you to improve and that you will do all you can in His power to make those improvements.**

Acknowledgments

I am passionate about training worship leaders globally to better lead their congregations in transformational worship. I am excited about the possibilities this book offers in reaching many more people with this curriculum developed over the last 20+ years. There are several people that God has used along the way specifically to encourage me and help shape the development of this book.

First, over 20 years ago, I received a phone call from **Mark Abernathy** of North Carolina Baptists on Missions asking me to take my church's worship team to lead a large gathering of missionaries and their families in worship for a week-long conference in Malaysia. Then, **Rodney Duncan**, a missionary in Malaysia, asked me to consider teaching worship conferences in Malaysia and Singapore during the second week following the conference. That was definitely out of my comfort zone and nothing I had done before. This "yes" answer forever changed my ministry. I continue to regularly take teams to that part of the world, leading worship conferences and other events while continually revising and contextualizing the curriculum we use.

God further used two pastors of the church I served as missions and worship pastor, Front Street Baptist Church in

Statesville, North Carolina, to encourage and develop me in the years I served with them. I learned so much from these men. **Gerald Bontrager** greatly helped me grow as a leader and encouraged my missions involvement. **Tim Stutts** was not only an encourager and great friend those years we served together but also has continued to be a close friend today with whom I have much interaction.

Many on the Front Street Baptist Church worship team took off work for many weeks to assist me in international missions work during my time there. I am so thankful for the sacrifices they made and the lives they impacted. The church also granted me a missions sabbatical that further shaped my life as I served a couple of months in Malaysia. In addition, many people from other churches in recent years have assisted me on these overseas trips and have a special place in my heart for their sacrificial service.

Brian Upshaw invited me to join the staff of the Baptist State Convention of North Carolina (BSCNC) thirteen years ago. He commented that working from the BSCNC platform would give me more significant opportunities to make a difference in thousands of lives of worship leaders. Working for North Carolina Baptists has been incredibly fulfilling and exciting in the organization's work in North Carolina and worldwide. Brian, a great friend and leader, continues to support me in many ways and has greatly helped me develop as a leader.

Another missionary who has been instrumental in my development as a trainer of worship leaders is **Michael Webber** (name changed for security reasons). Years ago, he invited me to come to his country at the request of the house church to train a select handful of young worship leaders over several successive years. That was perhaps the most fulfilling ministry work I have ever done—multiplying myself in a closed country and pouring into the lives of young Christians there. Those young men and women are dear to my heart, and I am so thankful for them (I would love to list their names here, but for security reasons, I cannot). Later Michael invited me to be a part of work happening in Cambodia, opening up so many new opportunities.

One such opportunity was to provide a book on worship for the Cambodian church. **Jeff Lai** of Action Cambodia encouraged me to create a stand-alone resource (book) to help the church there since there are no books on worship printed in Khmer. I was excited to be able to continue the work that was started there with a couple of weeks of conferences with the release of this book. I am so thankful for my interpreter in Cambodia, **Buntha Lee**, who has also lovingly translated the book manuscript into Khmer to prepare for publication. Once I prepared that manuscript, I moved on to preparing this book for English publication.

I offer a very special thanks to **Doris Henderson**, a lady who exemplifies serving God with all one has years after retirement. She lovingly spent hours editing this manuscript to help it communicate more powerfully.

Additionally, my friend, **David Manner**, was a tremendous guide and encourager through the process of writing this book. David is a great friend and author who has inspired me for years with his great wisdom and writing in the area of worship.

Special thanks go to the **Marketing and Communications Group** at the Baptist State Convention of North Carolina, who consistently exemplify excellence in everything they do and help me and my colleagues fulfill our calling with excellence.

They have taken this project and run with it to help me use it to minister to churches worldwide. I am especially indebted to my amazing book designer, **Carlee Hoopes**, who patiently worked with me to achieve the product you have in your hand.

One exceptional group in my life is comprised of my **counterparts from other Baptist state conventions.** We are a tight group of friends who work together to help our churches improve their worship times and support and encourage one another. This group is like family to me.

When it comes to accomplishing the task God has called me to, I must say I am blessed with an amazing ministry assistant, **Ethan Nunn**, who makes my life so much easier.

I am most thankful to **my wife, Sandy**, my best friend and life mate. Her support and love keep me going. She has had to put up with quite a bit in my travels and work, but she always makes our home a very special place to return to. I thank God for her! God has also blessed me with two wonderful children (**Kevin & Katie**), a wonderful daughter-in-law (**Zion**) and son-in-law (**Jonathan**), and now two amazing granddaughters (**Raelyn & Zoe**).

Most of all, I thank God for loving a sinner like me and putting up with all my flaws and missteps. He loves me unconditionally and leads me to exciting opportunities that bring great joy as I find the center of His will for my life.

I pray that God will use this book to help many worship leaders make a difference in the lives of their congregations by providing times of transformational worship.

NOTES

INTRODUCTION

1. John Piper, "Missions Exists Because Worship Doesn't," *Desiring God*, https://www.desiringgod.org/messages/missions-exists-because-worship-doesnt-a-bethlehem-legacy-inherited-and-bequeathed.
2. Chuck Swindoll, *The Church Awakening: An Urgent Call for Renewal* (United States: FaithWords, 2010), Kindle.
3. Constance M. Cherry, *The Worship Architect: A Blueprint for Designing Culturally Relevant and Biblically Faithful Services* (Grand Rapids: Baker, 2010), 270.
4. Constance M. Cherry, *The Worship Architect: A Blueprint for Designing Culturally Relevant and Biblically Faithful Services* (Grand Rapids: Baker, 2010), 270, as quoted in James Magaw, "The Power We Invoke," Alive Now (May-June 1988): 60, quoting Annie Dillard, Teaching a Stone to Talk: Expeditions and Encounters (New York: Harper Collins, 1982), 40-41.
5. James Magaw, "The Power We Invoke," Alive Now (May-June 1988) 60-61.

UNDERSTANDING WORSHIP

6. "Worship," *Merriam-Webster Online Dictionary*, https://www.merriam-webster.com/dictionary/worship.
7. Tim Keller, *Counterfeit Gods: The Empty Promises of Money, Sex, and Power, and the Only Hope That Matters* (Viking, 2009), xviii.
8. Harold Best, *Music Through the Eyes of Faith* (HarperOne, 1993), 143.
9. "Worship," Merriam-Webster Online Dictionary.
10. Michael Morrison, "What is Worship? A Survey of the Bible," *Grace Communion Seminary*, https://learn.gcs.edu/mod/page/view.php?id=4256.
11. "Proskuneo," *Bible Study Tools*, https://www.biblestudytools.com/lexicons/greek/kjv/proskuneo.html.
12. "Shachah," *Bible Tools*, https://www.bibletools.org/index.cfm/fuseaction/lexicon.show/ID/h7812/page/2.
13. John Piper, "What Is Worship," *Desiring God*, https://www.desiringgod.org/interviews/what-is-worship.
14. Warren Wiersbe, *Real Worship: It Will Tranform Your Life* (United States, Baker Publishing Group, 2000), 26.
15. Robert Schaper, *In His Presence: Appreciating Your Worship Tradition* (Nashville: T. Nelson Publishers), 15-16.
16. Stephen Brooks, *Worship Quest: An Exploration of Worship Leadership* (United States: Wipf and Stock Publishers, 2015), Kindle.

17. Michael Morrison.

18. Bob Kauflin, "Defining Worship, Pt.3," *Worship Matters*, https://worshipmatters.com/2005/11/08/defining-worship-part-3.

19. Bryan Chapell, *Christ-Centered Worship: Letting the Gospel Shape Our Practice* (United States: Baker Academic, 2017), 114-115.

20. Michael Morrison.

21. Richard Foster, *Celebration of Discipline: The Path to Spiritual Growth* (New York: HarperCollins, 1998) 173.

22. Steven Brooks.

23. The understanding of these four contexts primarily from the work of Syd Hielema and Paul Clark, Jr., and Steven Brooks. You will see endnotes for these resources elsewhere in the material.

24. Syd Hielema, "The Festival-Envy Syndrome: Four Contexts of Worship", Reformed Worship 71 (2004). Worship Ministries of the Reformed Church. Used by permission.

25. Jim Altizer, *The Making of a Worship Leader* (United States: Sound & Light Publishing, 2013), 52.

26. Paul B. Clark, Jr. *Tune My Heart to Sing Thy Grace: Worship Renewal Through Congregational Singing* (United States: Cross Books Publishing, 2010), 48-49.

27. Syd Hielema.

28. Rory Noland, *Worship on Earth As It Is in Heaven: Exploring Worship as a Spiritual Discipline*. (United States: Zondervan, 2011), Kindle.

29. Kierkegaard, Søren, trans. Douglas V. Steere. *Purity of Heart Is to Will One Thing* (New York: HarperCollins, 2008), 180-189.

30. Brian Crosby, "Participation in Worship", *TableTalk Magazine*, https://tabletalkmagazine.com/article/2022/01/participation-in-worship.

31. Steve Hamrick, Associate Pastor of Worship & Media, FBC Greenville, MS, Adjunct professor at William Carey University.

32. Ed Stetzer and Thom Rainer, *Transformational Church: Creating a New Scorecard for Congregations* (United States: B&H Publishing Group, 2010), 161.

33. Chuck Swindoll, *The Church Awakening: An Urgent Call for Renewal* (United States: FaithWords, 2010), Kindle.

34. Ibid.

35. Ibid.

36. Excerpted from a document from First Baptist Church, Durham, NC. Used by permission.

37. Chuck Swindoll.

38. Ibid.

39. C. S. Lewis, "Answers to Questions on Christianity," in *God in the Dock: Essays on*

Theology and Ethics (Grand Rapids: Eerdmans, 1970], 51–52.

40. Tullian Tchividjian, *Unfashionable: Making a Difference in the World by Being Different* (United States: Crown Publishing Group, 2012), Kindle.

41. Jim Bradford, in a letter written to his congregation at Central Assembly of God in Springfield, Missouri. Dr. Bradford graciously gave me permission to include his letter in this book.

42. Henry Blackaby, Richard Blackaby. *Flickering Lamps: Christ and His Church.* (United States: Blackaby Ministries International), 2015.

43. Chuck Lawless, "10 Leadership Mistakes in Transitioning a Church," *Chuck Lawless: Evangelism, Leadership, Missiology, Church Health,* https://chucklawless.com/2015/10/10-leadership-mistakes-in-transitioning-a-church.

44. Graham Kendrick, unknown source.

45. Chuck Swindoll.

46. David Manner, "Are You Leading Worship Change with a Wrecking Ball? Try Deconstruction," *Worship Evaluation,* http://WorshipEvaluation.org/are-you-leading-worship-change-with-a-wrecking-ball-try-deconstruction/.

UNDERSTANDING WORSHIP LEADERSHIP

47. David Manner, "Is Change Necessary? Then Burn Your Boats," *Worship Evaluation,* http://WorshipEvaluation.org/is-change-necessary-then-burn-your-boats/.

48. Jeff Iorg, *Is God Calling Me?: Answering the Question Every Believer Asks* (Nashville: B&H Publishing Group, 2008).

49. Ibid, 20.

50. Henry Blackaby and Claude King, *Experiencing God: Knowing and Doing the Will of God* (United States: B&H Publishing Group, 2008) 57.

51. Bob Kauflin, "6 Reasons Worship Leaders Should Be Musical Pastors," *ChurchLeaders.com,* https://churchleaders.com/worship/worship-articles/253170-call-musical-pastors.html/2.

52. Brenton Collyer, "How to Increase Engagement in Your Worship Services," *Worship Ministry Training Podcast,* https://www.worshipministrytraining.com/how-to-increase-engagement-in-your-worship-services/.

53. John Piper, "What Unites Us in Worship," *DesiringGod.org,* https://www.desiringgod.org/articles/what-unites-us-in-worship.

54. David Santistevan, "7 Disciplines of a Good Worship Leader," *Beyond Sunday Worship,* https://www.davidsantistevan.com/7-disciplines-of-a-good-worship-leader/.

55. Ibid.

56. A.W. Tozer, *The Knowledge of the Holy: The Attributes of God, Their Meaning in the Christian Life* (United Kingdom: Clarke, 1965), Kindle.

57. Zac Hicks. *The Worship Pastor: A Call to Ministry for Worship Leaders and Teams* (United States: Zondervan, 2016) Kindle.

58. Ibid.

59. Rory Noland, *The Heart of the Artist: A Character-Building Guide for You and Your Ministry Team* (United States, Zondervan, 2009), Kindle.

60. Jon Nichols seeks to help worship leaders equip a strong team that leads engaging worship through online classes, resources, mentoring and much more. You can learn more at his website, WorshipTeamCoach.com.

PLANNING WORSHIP

61. Adapted from Pastor Scott Christensen's document, *How to Evaluate Songs for Congregational Worship*. Summit Lake Community Church, Mancos, Colorado.

62. Mike Harland, *"Can We Sing 'Their' Songs," Renewing Worship*, https://www.renewingworshipnc.org/can-we-sing-their-songs.

63. Ibid.

64. David Manner in a comment placed on Kenny Lamm's blog post, "Should My Church Sing Songs from Bethel and Hillsong?" *Renewing Worship.* https://www.renewingworshipnc.org/should-my-church-sings-songs-from-bethel-hillsong-and-elevation-church.

65. Don Chapman, "Linking Praise Songs," *WorshipIdeas*, https://www.worshipideas.com/linking-praise-songs.

66. Constance Cherry, *The Music Architect: Blueprints for Engaging Worshipers in Song* (United States, Baker Publishing Group, 2016), 60.

67. James White, *Introduction to Christian Worship*, 3rd ed. (Nashville: Abingdon, 2000), 114.

68. I read this years ago in a book but cannot locate the source.

69. John Piper, *Desiring God: Meditations of a Christian Hedonist* (United States: Multnomah Books, 1996), 81-82.

70. I heard this in a sermon years ago, source unknown.

71. Steven Brooks, *Worship Quest*, 76.

LEADING WORSHIP

72. Kenny Lamm, "9 Reasons People Aren't Singing in Worship," *Renewing Worship*, https://www.renewingworshipnc.org/nine-reasons-people-arent-singing-in-worship. Some ideas for the opening paragraphs of this article come from David Murrow's article, *Why men have stopped singing in church*. https://www.patheos.

com/blogs/churchformen/2013/05/why-men-have-stopped-singing-in-church/.

73. Alex Enfiedjian, "Eight Tricks to Improve Your Stage Presence," *WorshipMinistryTraining.com*, https://www.worshipministrytraining.com/8-tricks-to-improve-your-stage-presence.

74. Dave Williamson, *God's Singers: A Guidebook for the Worship Leading Choir in the 21st Century* (United States: In:Ciite Media, 2010) 124.

DOWNLOAD A FREE
group study
**TO ACCOMPANY
THIS BOOK AT**

WORSHIPMINISTRYGUIDEBOOK.COM

Made in the USA
Middletown, DE
04 September 2024

60290715R00157